WHY IS CHRISTIANITY SO HARD?

WHY IS CHRISTIANITY SO HARD?

Michael F. Annanie

ELM HILL

A Division of
HarperCollins Christian Publishing

www.elmhillbooks.com

Why Is Christianity So Hard?

Published in Nashville, Tennessee, by Elm Hill, an imprint of Thomas Nelson. Elm Hill and Thomas Nelson are registered trademarks of HarperCollins Christian Publishing, Inc.

Elm Hill titles may be purchased in bulk for educational, business, fund-raising, or sales promotional use. For information, please e-mail SpecialMarkets@ ThomasNelson.com.

Library of Congress Cataloging-in-Publication Data

Library of Congress Control Number: 2020900940

ISBN 978-1-400330973 (Paperback)
ISBN 978-1-400330966 (Hardbound)
ISBN 978-1-400330980 (eBook)

ACKNOWLEDGEMENT

To the Holy Spirit who taught me everything I know that is worth knowing. To Jesus Christ who saved me from my sins and restored the relationship with God the Father. To God, who loved me.

To my stepmom, Miriam, who saved me from my teenage years and showed me how to live life.

To my wife who loves me unconditionally.

To my three children who have taught me more than I have taught them.

To all those that encouraged, taught and walked with me in this faith journey, I will be forever thankful.

PREFACE

"Why is Christianity So Hard?" was written for those that are struggling with faith because it wasn't what they expected. They found it to be too hard, contradictory or confusing. Many expect it to be like we had it in the Garden of Eden. There is an expectation that Christianity was going to be a blissful easy life. When they find out that we live in a fallen world, then they quit without fully understanding why.

When I have asked folks if they think Christianity is hard, I have received a very high response rate that it is hard. Yes, there are some that find Christianity easy. God love them. That is not my experience.

Christianity is hard because you must want it with all your heart, mind and soul. God wants all of us. He doesn't want half-hearted disciples. This book is written to encourage folks that following Christ is not only worthwhile but is the only way to live life.

This book addresses the questions posed by those that God brought into my life. And the questions that I have asked myself. For example, if God made the Gospel message so simple, why is it that so many don't believe? God has given us a choice and is willing to let us live with our choice. Even if that means not choosing Him. We must choose to follow Christ with every decision.

This book explores the tensions in the Christian faith and the difficulty of following Jesus as His disciple. There is a conundrum in the Christian faith. On the one hand, salvation is a gift of God, *"For by grace you have been saved through faith, and that not of yourselves; it is the gift of*

God." (Ephesians 2:8 NKJV) It is to be received freely. We can do nothing to earn it. God couldn't have made it easier. Christ did everything for us.

On the other hand, to be a disciple of Christ and follow him, we are to suffer, deny ourselves, and pick up our cross daily. Jesus commands us to follow Him, "*And he who does not take his cross and follow after Me is not worthy of Me.*" (Matthew 10:38 NKJV) To follow Jesus and be His disciple takes everything including our life. So, which is it?

Jesus tells us to calculate the costs prior to committing to be a disciple. (Luke 14:27-33 NKJV). This book enables those to calculate the cost of discipleship. It also enables those to calculate the cost of not deciding to follow Christ. The choice is real with eternal consequences.

This book takes a unique approach to looking at faith that I haven't seen elsewhere. That Christianity is hard. Following Christ and being His disciple is hard until you figure out to yield to the Holy Spirit, let Christ live through you and rest in God's love. We need to get ourselves out of the way and let God work through us. It is only by the grace of God that we can do anything. Which is in and of itself very difficult (at least for me) to do consistently with every decision.

God has pressed me to write this book for at least 10 years. I am not sure what He wants to do with it. I am just being obedient in writing the book.

My heart is that you find this book encouraging and leads you to a richer and deeper love of Jesus Christ.

Sit Gratia Domini Iesu Christi vobiscum
(May the Grace of our Lord Jesus Christ be with you).

TABLE OF CONTENTS

CHAPTER 1

GOD IS ABLE.
DO YOU BELIEVE IT?

"But without faith it is impossible to please Him, for he who comes to God must believe that He is, and that He is a rewarder of those who diligently seek Him."

(HEB 11:6 NKJV)

Christianity is hard because it takes faith. Many people want to know God is real before they will believe. They want to base their faith on knowledge. Faith doesn't work that way. It is backwards to how our culture thinks and processes information. We must believe first and then we will know. We must *"believe that He is."* (Heb 11:6 NKJV) This is one of the reasons that faith is so hard for many people.

For that reason, there will be a lot of smart people in hell. They thought they knew better. They were afraid or didn't want to believe. The Gospel defies all common sense. It makes no sense. It is foolishness to those that are perishing, *"For the message of the cross is foolishness to those who are perishing, but to us who are being saved it is the power of God."* (1 Corinthians 1:18 NKJV) They want to know and then they will believe. The message of the cross is hard to believe for those who have hardened their hearts, for those who want to know first.

Seeking God without seeing Him or knowing He exists is how we find Him. Through wisdom, the world tries to know God. The finished work of Jesus on the cross is foolishness to those of worldly wisdom. The proud and wise of this world are unwilling to surrender their wisdom and submit to God. The foolish thing is that they are holding onto something that is perishable. Faith is believing in something that is eternal.

Humans have tried since Christ lived on earth to prove He either isn't real or He didn't really live, or He isn't really God. All the efforts of humans to "know" has only proven that Jesus is real. There are many examples of people trying to know. There are archeological digs, historical analysis, and attempts to prove inconsistencies or contradictions in the Bible. And yet Jesus and the Bible lives. And people still believe.

We search and read the Bible looking for answers that will help us know so then we can believe. We are looking to know for sure. We are looking for some evidence that will convince us, and then we will believe. If we begin with believing and step out on that faith, then we will begin to know. When we read the Bible with faith, the Word will penetrate our heart and change us. Head knowledge will only take us so far in our relationship with Jesus. It is a matter of the heart. It takes faith to know God. There is a difference between knowing and believing. We must believe that He is; then we will know.

Paul warns Timothy of those who are "*always learning and never able to come to the knowledge of the truth.*" (2 Tim 3:7 NKJV) And people struggle with faith "*Because they did not seek it by faith, but as it were, by the works of the law. For they stumbled at that stumbling stone.*" (Rom 9:32 NKJV) The stumbling stone is Jesus.

Christianity is hard because head knowledge will cause us to have weakened faith from time to time. God gives us the ways to "know Him." He gives us the Spirit to know Him and believe in Him. The onus is on us to answer His call. To accept His free gift of salvation. The Spirit will work on our hearts and minds. God put the knowledge in our hearts to know Him, so we are without excuse. "*For since the creation of the world His invisible attributes are clearly seen, being understood by the things that* are made, even His eternal power and Godhead, so that they are without excuse because, although they knew God, they did not glorify Him as God, nor were thankful, but became futile in their thoughts, and their foolish hearts were darkened." (Rom 1:20–21 NKJV)

The Bible illustrates the difference between knowing and believing in the book of Luke. (Luke 8:49–56 NKJV) This is the story of Jesus healing Jairus's daughter. Jesus has compassion on the ruler and goes to revive his daughter. Jesus states to "only believe" in verse 50, "Do not be afraid; only believe and she will be made well." As Jesus enters the house and sees the people crying, He says, "Do not weep; she is not dead, but sleeping." (Luke 8:52 NKJV) But the people "knew" better and didn't believe Him. They ridiculed Jesus in verse 53, "And they ridiculed Him, knowing that she was dead." So, even after Jesus stated to only believe, people thought they knew better. It would have been difficult to believe that Jesus would be able to bring her back from death. How many times in life do we "know" that something is a done deal or the outcome is for certain? Our knowledge limits our ability to believe the impossible. With Jesus, all things are possible. Maybe we need to only believe. This section of the Bible is a real challenge to believe regardless of what the circumstances or situation is telling us. God is bigger than our circumstances. Do we believe it?

We can only hope that after Jesus healed Jairus's daughter, the people believed. That they believed Jesus after witnessing His works. They witnessed a miracle and Jesus' healing powers. In this verse, Jesus is talking to the people during His ministry about believing so that they may know, "If I do not do the works of My Father, do not believe Me; but if I do, though you do not believe Me, believe the works, that you may know and believe that the Father is in Me, and I in Him." (John 10:37–38 NKJV)

They had the unique privilege of seeing the works of Jesus and still struggled to believe that Jesus is God. They thought they knew better. This can happen to us today. We think we know better. We can still "see" the works of Jesus today. Answered prayer is an example of God working in our life. If we realize that it is God working in our lives and see the answered prayers, then we will know. God is able, do we believe it?

Some won't ever come to faith even if someone is raised from the dead. As the rich man in hell pleads, "*And he said, 'No, father Abraham; but if one goes to them from the dead, they will repent.' But he said to him, 'If they do not hear Moses and the prophets, neither will they be persuaded though one rise from the dead.'*" (Luke 16:30–31 NKJV) Jesus rose from the dead to defeat sin and death. Who will believe it?

Christianity is hard because faith is either growing or fading away. Faith must be fed and nurtured or it will fade away to nothing. If we don't use our faith, then it will dissipate and our faith will fall away. Keeping our faith strong requires a daily choice to follow Christ.

Faith grows more faith. Exercising our faith strengthens our faith. Which in turn causes us to trust more. Which then gives us the confidence to step out again on faith. An effective way to strengthen our faith is to make a memory of God working in our life.

The Bible provides an example of making a memory in the book of Joshua. God instructed Joshua to make a memorial of His faithfulness. When the nation of Israel crossed the Jordan into the promised land, God parted the Jordan for them. They crossed on dry land. God instructed Joshua to have twelve men grab twelve big stones from the river bottom and take them to the other side. There they set up a memorial to remind the children of Israel.

And when the children would ask, "*What do these stones mean to you? Then you shall answer them that the waters of the Jordan were cut off before the ark of the covenant of the* LORD; *when it crossed over the Jordan, the waters of the Jordan were cut off. And these stones shall be for a memorial to the children of Israel forever.*" (Joshua 4:6–7 NKJV)

We can apply this to our life. We can and should make memories of when we <u>know</u> that God had worked in our life or provided answer to a prayer. There was no other explanation of how the problem was solved. That way, when our faith is weakened, and we are being tossed to and fro (James 1:6 NKJV), we can remember back to when God was faithful and use it to strengthen our faith. He will be faithful again. Do we believe it?

Another benefit of making memorial stones is that it will be an example to others. Later in Joshua, the Bible explains that "*all the peoples of the earth may know the hand of the LORD, that it is mighty, that you may fear the LORD your God forever.*" (Joshua 4:24 NKJV) We may not be aware of the impact our faith has on other people around us.

Make a pile of stones. Make memories of the faithfulness of God. Hold onto those memories; cherish them, use them to strengthen our faith. "*God is faithful, by whom you were called into the fellowship of His Son, Jesus Christ our Lord.*" (1 Cor 1:9 NKJV)

Christianity is hard because it is a matter of the heart. Faith (and knowing) is a matter of the heart. A heart for God: "*Then I will give them a heart to know Me, that I am the LORD; and they shall be My people, and I will be their God, for they shall return to Me with their whole heart.*" (Jer 24:7 NKJV)

The condition of the heart is important. A softened heart will receive the Word of God. A hardened heart keeps people from believing and eventually knowing. A hardened heart refuses to let the Word of God sink into the heart. Earthly circumstances harden the heart and impact the ability to believe. Possessions, people, things, and worry can harden a person's heart. We think we know better. There were times when we thought we knew better. It was unthinkable that God would care about us or our situation. We have trouble believing because we thought we knew for sure what was going to happen. Instead of believing, we thought. This is a matter of the heart and not the mind.

Only by relying on faith can one truly understand and know God. After Jesus feeds the five thousand, Mark states that the disciples have hardened hearts keeping them from believing. "*For they had not understood about the loaves, because their heart was hardened.*" (Mark 6:52) Jesus continues this line of thought for the disciples in the eighth chapter of Mark, "*But Jesus, being aware of it, said to them, 'Why do you reason because you have no bread? Do you not yet perceive nor understand? Is your heart still hardened?'*" (Mark 8:17 NKJV) It is important to have a soft heart to be able to receive the Word of God. The writer of Hebrews cautions against hardening our heart: "*While it is said: 'Today, if you will hear His voice, Do not harden your hearts as in the rebellion.' And this leads to the logical conclusion—lack of faith."* (Hebrews 3:15 NKJV) and the result is unbelief, *"So we see that they could not enter in because of unbelief."* (Hebrews 3:19 NKJV)

The Word of God reveals what is in our hearts. The writer of Hebrews states that the Word of God is a discerner of the thoughts and intents of the heart, *"For the word of God is living and powerful, and sharper than any two-edged sword, piercing even to the division of soul and spirit, and of joints and marrow, and is a discerner of the thoughts and intents of the heart."* (Heb 4:12 NKJV)

There is a difference between believing and knowing. Faith is defined as *"the substance of things hoped for, the evidence of things not seen."* (Heb 11:1 NKJV) This verse doesn't say anything about knowing. To believe God without knowing makes us rely on him and is a true testament of faith. Because if we knew, then it wouldn't be faith. We must believe.

An example of believing and still wanting to know is Abram. He starts with believing, *"And he believed in the LORD, and He accounted it to him for righteousness."* (Gen 15:6 NKJV) We as a people have always struggled with the question Abram poses next, *"Lord God, how shall I know that I will inherit it?"* (Gen 15:8 NKJV) Even though Abram had believed God, he still wanted to know.

Waiting and relying on God makes Christianity difficult for many people. We like to plan. We like to know the outcome prior to moving forward. With Christ, we must wait on Him. We must rely on His strength, power, and wisdom. We can't rely on our own skills. We must live through Christ. We must move forward without knowing; only believing that Christ has the best for us.

So then, how does God answer Abram? God gives him a vision in his sleep and makes a covenant with him. He tells him in a dream, *"Know certainly that your…."* (Gen 15:13a NKJV) Better make a memory of that dream. Set up a pile of stones.

Abram's son learns what it is to know God in the story of Jacob's ladder. God sets up a ladder for Jacob. This ladder reaches to the heavens and has angels going up and down on it. And there was the Lord at the top of the ladder. He says, *"I am the Lord...."* (Gen 28:13 NKJV) And he gives Jacob instructions on how his life is going to proceed. What a blessing to know that God has talked to us and told us that He was going to be with us. Wow! Now, what was Jacob's response? He stated, *"Surely the LORD is in this place, and I did not know it."* (Gen 28:16 NKJV) How many times the Lord is in a place and we don't know it. We need to look for the Lord. We need to be attuned to the Holy Spirit. If we aren't seeking God, we will never know that He is with us. When we find that God is working in our life (notice that it is when and not if), we should rejoice like Jacob does, *"How awesome is this place! This is none other than the house of God, and this is the gate of heaven!"* (Gen 28:17 NKJV)

An important action by Jacob is to mark the moment. Too often God makes a mark on our life and we don't stop to make a memory. It is those memories that we can look back on and remember that the Lord is working in our life. He has worked in our life in the past and He will work in our life in the future. It helps us when our faith is weak. And then Jacob's final response should always be the ultimate response and the one that is pleasing to the Lord, *"Then the LORD shall be my God."* (Gen 28:21 NKJV)

How many times do we not have the faith that God will perform a work in our lives? (See the chapter Living in Anticipation for details about answered prayer.) If we only had the faith to trust God, then we would get to know God more. This process feeds on itself in both directions. The more we trust and believe God, the more we see Him active in our lives. The more we don't trust Him, the easier it is for us to fade away and stop believing.

In the Old Testament, God continues to perform miracles and signs that His people will finally know that He is Lord. He tries many things to make His people acknowledge Him and love Him. But they would continue to turn away from Him. This is how many operate today.

Hebrews goes on to say in verse 11:3, *"By faith we understand...."* It goes on to tell us that the worlds were framed by the word of God. But in short, it is by faith that we understand the mysteries of God. It is only by faith can we understand or know God. If we want to know God, then we must first believe that He is the great I AM.

The more we trust and walk in faith, the more we will know. God will prove faithful and show up in our life. God wants all of us to come to a saving knowledge of Jesus Christ, *"For this is good and acceptable in the sight of God our Savior, who desires all men to be saved and to come to the knowledge of the truth."* (1 Tim 2:3–4 NKJV)

The Lord has provided us the Word for us to know Him. The more that we live and walk in (obey) His Word, the more we will know Him. Pray that we will know the Lord today by believing that He is, *"And this is eternal life, that they may know You, the only true God, and Jesus Christ whom You have sent."* (John 17:3 NKJV)

Paul sought knowledge to the extent that he counted all things as a loss to gain knowledge of Jesus Christ, *"Yet indeed I also count all things loss for the excellence of the knowledge of Christ Jesus my Lord."* (Philippians 3:8 NKJV)

Are you trying to know or are you willing to believe?

Devotional – Scoring Big at Christmas

When I was little, gifts made Christmas. For weeks leading up to Christmas, we (my siblings and I) would venture to dream about the gifts and the excitement of opening the gifts. We dreamed of scoring big at Christmas.

The gifts or the thoughts of gifts have changed for me. A few years back during one Christmas season, I realized that I had the best gift already: the gift of God, Jesus Christ. And how everything else pales in comparison.

There are many verses in the Bible about gifts. Ecclesiastes 3 NKJV says, *"For a man to enjoy the good of all his labor is a gift of God."* Matthew 7 says, *"How much more will your Father who is in heaven give good things to those who ask Him!"* Romans 5 states that it is a free gift. 1 Corinthians

12 and Ephesians 4 describe the various gifts and talents that God bestows on us. Romans 6 tells us the gift of God is eternal life in Christ Jesus, our Lord.

There is one catch about gifts, though: you must accept them for them to be yours.

The way to score big at Christmas is to accept Jesus as your Lord and Savior. To believe that He is. I pray that you accept the gift of God and that you will know Jesus, the Savior of the world.

CHAPTER 2

CHOICE

"Choose for yourselves this day whom you will serve, but as for me and my house, we will serve the Lord."

(JOSHUA 24:15 NKJV)

Faith is a choice. Love is a choice. Sin is a choice.

Christianity is hard because God gives us a choice to believe or not. God created man in his own image and likeness. He has given man the freedom to make choices. We can choose to believe that God exists or that He doesn't. God doesn't force the choice on us. Faith is the choice to believe in God, that He exists and that He is alive today. Faith is a choice that is made without knowing, only believing. God's love for His creation allows us to make our own choices.

Christianity is hard because God will let us have our way. If a creator wants His creation to love Him, then the creator has two options. First, He could build the creation to love Him. Or as a second option, He could leave the choice up to the creation. We are living with the second option. We have a choice. God's desire is for us to love Him back. He loves us enough to give us the choice. He loves us enough to let us have our way.

In the first option, the creation is more robotic in its responses. Programmed to love Him. That is not true love. That is programmed love.

Of course, the creation loves Him; it was created with no choice but to love the creator. Humans were given the choice to love or not. When a created being has a choice to love or not and decides to love, then that is true love. Especially if it costs them something. There is no satisfaction that the creation really loves God back with the first option.

The second option is better in that the creation has the choice and still decides to love the creator. It is very similar to the parent-children relationship. Children don't have to love their parents. The kids could rebel and move away at the earliest opportunity. Any parent who has had a prodigal child knows all too well how much that hurts. We can only imagine how much God feels as the Father when His children rebel. But if the kids choose to stay and love their parents back, it is very sweet, and we know that it is a true love. They honor their parents with their love just as we should honor God with our love.

God wants us to choose to love Him. That is the relationship we had with Him in the Garden of Eden. He has continually throughout history tried to get us to love Him on our own. God wants us to love Him. He could force us to love Him, but He doesn't. Love is so much better if it is a willing love. That is why we have the choice to accept the Lord or not. For if we love Him of our own will, then the chances that the love will last is much greater. When we choose to love the Lord, then it is our choice. That means that we truly love Him for who He is and not because we are forced to or because of what He can do for us.

For any choice to be a real choice, there must something to choose between. There must be at least two clear options. Enter the prince of this world, Satan (Eph 2:2, Jn 14:30 NKJV) Satan is real. Please don't underestimate the power that Satan wields in this present earth. He may ask for the ability to test us like he did with Job (Job 1:9-12 NKJV) Or sift us as wheat, like he did with Peter (Luke 22:31 NKJV) Satan wants to keep us from knowing and loving God. His work started in the Garden of Eden when Adam and Eve ate of the tree of knowledge of good and evil (Gen 3:4-5 NKJV) And he continues his work to this day. His job is to separate us from God, to give us a real choice.

For there to be a real choice, then hell must also be real. Discipline and Judgment must be as real as a loving God and His Son Jesus Christ. There needs to be consequences to the choice. People want it both ways. They want to live in the flesh and follow all their fleshy ways. And they want to be forgiven and taken back as a son or daughter. The second part takes true repentance. Not just a regret that we were caught. It takes following Christ. Loving Him with our whole heart. Placing Him first in our life.

God will respect our choice. He loves us so much that He will give us our hearts' desire, even if it is to not love Him back. God will let us go to the devil, *"Deliver such a one to Satan for the destruction of the flesh, that his spirit may be saved in the day of the Lord Jesus."* (1 Corinthians 5:5 NKJV) We should always remind ourselves of the other side of the choice. Many folks don't fully think through the decision. They can only see what is in front of them and not the eternal consequences. Jesus is enough. Do we believe it?

Christianity is hard because Satan, the adversary, is constantly trying to pull us away from God. Satan was created and was one of the chosen. Pride caused his fall from Heaven, *"How you are fallen from heaven, O Lucifer, son of the morning! How you are cut down to the ground, You who weakened the nations! For you have said in your heart: 'I will ascend into heaven, I will exalt my throne above the stars of God.'"* (Isaiah 14:12–13a NKJV) He is the ruler of this earthly world. (Jn 14:30 NKJV) His demons, which are many, do his work for him. (Mark 5:9 NKJV) Satan is seeking to devour us, *"Be sober, be vigilant; because your adversary the devil walks about like a roaring lion, seeking whom he may devour."* (1 Peter 5:8 NKJV)

Every day with every choice, it's a decision to choose between God and Satan. We can either choose to glorify God or we can choose to glorify Satan. This is what the Bible means when it says to live by the flesh or live by the Spirit. *"There is therefore now no condemnation to those who are in Christ Jesus, who do not walk according to the flesh, but according to the Spirit."* (Romans 8:1 NKJV) To walk according to the flesh is to walk according to this world and the ruler of it, Satan. By not accepting Christ, we are making a choice for Satan.

The daily choices aren't talking about the choice to accept Christ. That is made once, and it is a done deal. The cross is enough. It is talking about picking up our cross daily and following Christ, *"If anyone desires to come after Me, let him deny himself, and take up his cross daily, and follow Me"* (Lk 9:23 NKJV) Daily we are to take up our cross. All day long we're given choices. And in those choices do we follow Christ or do we follow Satan. We ought to choose to follow Christ. This is very difficult for Christians. Choosing Christ all the time battles against the flesh. We fail often. We make bad decisions that don't follow Christ. The flesh is strong, and the desire is intense. This is one of the main reasons that Christianity is hard. It takes a complete commitment to follow Christ.

Each time before we sin, there is a choice. The choice is whether to obey the spirit or the flesh. As a temptation presents itself, and we dwell on it, sin presents itself, *"But each one is tempted when he is drawn away by his own desires and enticed. Then, when desire has conceived, it gives birth to sin; and sin, when it is full-grown, brings forth death."* (James 1:14–15 NKJV) At that point, we need to understand that this is a decision. The Tempter, Satan himself, presents many lies that make sinning seem very appealing. His appeals to our human nature; pride, self, pleasure, greed, why not me? He tries to convince us that we deserve it. But it still a choice.

Sometimes we don't know that we are sinning. There are cases when we aren't aware that what we did was a sin. There are cases where we don't know we have an idol that takes precedence before the Lord. As we proceed through sanctification, God reveals to us through His Spirit areas of our life that we need to release to Him. We didn't know that we had an idol that was taking precedence before the Lord. There are sins in our lives that God reveals to us as we mature in the faith and grow closer to Him.

Christianity is hard because a believer is constantly faced with choices. The choice is whether to be with God or be with Satan. Faith takes a daily choice to follow Jesus all day long. When we love someone, we want to follow them, *"But whoever keeps His word, truly the love of God is perfected in him. By this we know that we are in Him."* (1 John 2:5

NKJV) Jesus asks us to follow Him. (Matt 16:24 NKJV) It is ironic that we know what trips us up in sin. We know our weak points. We also know Satan's tactics, *"lest Satan should take advantage of us; for we are not ignorant of his devices"* (2 Corinthians 2:11 NKJV) Yet his tactics still work when we rely on our own strength.

Christianity is hard because God gave us freewill. In that freedom, man can choose to belief or not. God is willing to let us choose to love Him or not. He could have created us to love Him. In Mark, God's reaction to our choices is captured in a return visit to where Jesus grew up. (Mark 6:1–6 NKJV) The folks who have known Him as a boy are skeptical of His powers and wisdom. They don't believe. Jesus marvels at their unbelief, *"And He marveled because of their unbelief. Then He went about the villages in a circuit, teaching."* (Mark 6:6 NKJV) Because Jesus gives us the choice, He marvels when we choose to not accept Him nor believe in Him. He doesn't perform as many healings and miracles because of their choice to not believe.

The following example from the Bible shows where Peter had a choice to make. In the book of Luke, Jesus tells Peter, *"And the Lord said, "Simon, Simon! Indeed, Satan has asked for you, that he may sift you as wheat."* (Luke 22:31 NKJV) Being sifted as wheat doesn't sound very good. Peter-Simon will make a choice. And then Jesus tells Peter that He has prayed for him, *"But I have prayed for you, that your faith should not fail, ..."* (Luke 22:32 NKJV) Here the Lord prays that his faith wouldn't fail him. That he would make the choice to not follow Satan but follow Jesus. It is a day-in-and-day-out choice. Most of us would rather have the Lord just tell us that He fixed it. That He told Satan to leave Peter alone. But God works through faith. He wants us to believe first.

Christianity is hard because men add religious requirements to the Gospel. Here in this passage Jesus was rebuking the lawyers who were adding requirements to the Gospel, *"Woe to you lawyers! For you have taken away the key of knowledge. You did not enter in yourselves, and those who were entering in you hindered."* (Luke 11: 52 NKJV) Most of the religious requirements are man's attempt to help others with the choice. Unfortunately, the additional requirements often confuse the issue of choice, add nothing to the finished work of Jesus, and make people fall away from the faith.

How can the lawyers take away the key of knowledge? What is the key of knowledge that Jesus talks about here? It is the Gospel. The simple message of faith. They make it difficult for people to have the simple faith that Jesus and God want and desire. They add religious requirements that don't add to faith or exhort the Christian. Instead they bog the Christian down in traditions and false teachings that the Christian becomes discouraged and *"make him twice as much a son of hell as yourselves."* (Matt 23:15b NKJV) The lawyers made a choice to cherish their earthly life over a life with Christ.

The Pharisees also made a choice. The story in John about a man born blind that was healed by Jesus (John 9:1–41 NKJV) highlights the Pharisees' choice. The Pharisees had hardened their hearts and feared losing their current lifestyle. Therefore, they did not believe in this miracle. They struggled with what they knew and not what could be the truth. They needed to be willing to let go of their lives to be able to believe. They didn't want to believe that a man who was blind could be saved and teach them. The blind man began to teach the Pharisees. They were indignant because who was he to teach them because they knew so much from all their studies. Faith is a simple process and to know the Lord takes a simple heart and faith. Faith is too simple for people who want to know. The Pharisees were not open to the truth. Besides their own unbelief, they scared the Jews into not saying anything publicly about Jesus.

We must be willing to lose our life to be able to hear the truth. The Pharisees made a choice to not believe. In contrast, John the Baptist was willing to diminish so that Jesus could increase. We must be willing to lose our life so that we can gain Christ. This is the attitude that we must obtain. We cannot cling to our lives when it comes to hearing the Word of God and obeying.

Christianity is hard because we know good and evil. Man has strived to know the difference ever since the first bad choice. Knowledge of good and evil was promised to Adam and Eve if they would only sin and disobey God, *"Then the serpent said to the woman, 'You will not surely die. For God knows that in the day you eat of it your eyes will be opened, and you will be like God, knowing good and evil.'"* (Genesis 3:4–5 NKJV) Knowing good and evil is different from knowing the difference between good and evil. Discernment is knowing the difference. We need discernment to make wise choices.

Solomon asked for discernment above all else, *"'Therefore give to Your servant an understanding heart to judge Your people, that I may discern between good and evil. For who is able to judge this great people of Yours?' The speech pleased the LORD, that Solomon had asked this thing."* (1 Kings 3:9 NKJV) Spending time in God's word will provide discernment. Seek God by reading His word every day and we will start to understand Him, and therefore know Him. Reading our Bible is key to spiritual growth. It also aids in discerning between good and evil, *"But solid food belongs to those who are of full age, that is, those who by reason of use have their senses exercised to discern both good and evil."* (Hebrews 5:14 NKJV)

Opting not to choose is a choice. It is important to understand the impact of not choosing. In Proverbs, God explains to us that there are consequences for not choosing to fear the Lord. *"Then they will call on me, but I will not answer; They will seek me diligently, but they will not find me. Because they hated knowledge. And did not choose the fear of the LORD, They would have none of my counsel. And despised my every rebuke."* (Proverbs 1:28–30 NKJV) We make choices every day, all day long. God gives us free will to do as we please. How we choose then becomes very important. Understanding the consequences becomes even more important. If we do not listen when the Lord is disciplining us and trying to get us to turn back to Him, then He may not listen when we finally realize our need of Him. This is what happens when we don't respond to his discipline. He must have rebuked this group of people and they would not listen.

Christianity is hard because there are consequences to sin. Yes, Christ's work on the cross forgave all our sins. But there remains a consequence.

The Bible illustrates this point in 2 Sam 12 NKJV. Here David had sinned against the Lord by taking Bathsheba to be his wife and killing her husband Uriah (v9). Once Nathan makes this point with David, David repents and the Lord forgives David, *"The LORD also has put away your* sin; you shall not die" (v13). But there are still consequences to the sin. For David there were three consequences. First is "*the sword shall never depart from your house*" (v10); the second is "*I will take your wives before your eyes and give them to your neighbor, and he shall lie with your wives in the sight of this sun*" (v11); and the third is "*the child also who is born to you shall surely die*" (v14). All three of the consequences David lived with the rest of his life.

David made a choice that gave Satan a chance to gloat, "*However, because by this deed, you have given great occasion to the enemies of the LORD to blaspheme*" (V14). David was a man after God's own heart. He was the favored son of God. God explained the situation clearly to David, "*I gave you your master's house and your master's wives into your keeping and gave you the house of Israel and Judah. And if that had been too little, I also would have given you much more! Why have you despised the commandment of the LORD, to do evil in His sight?*" (v8-9) God is a loving Father who desires for His people to follow Him. He wants us to love Him by following Him. When we choose to follow Satan and not follow God, there is a consequence. He loves us enough to give us the choice. But He also loves us enough to correct us when we make bad choices, "*For whom the LORD loves He chastens, And scourges every son whom He receives.*" (Hebrews 12:6 NKJV)

Christianity is hard because we want it both ways. We want to act however we want, ignore the message and love of God, and then still have God come solve all our problems. It doesn't work that way, "*for if we sin willfully after we have received the knowledge of the truth, there no longer remains a sacrifice for sins, but a certain fearful expectation of judgment, and fiery indignation which will devour the adversaries.*" (Hebrews 10:26–27 NKJV) Willful describes an intentional and deliberate act of sin. There is no fear in a willful disobedience. God will execute justice. He marvels at our willful disobedience and obstinance. God will save us if we humble ourselves and repent, but there are consequences to our choices.

Many folks say that if God is all-loving, all-knowing, and all-powerful, why does He allow evil in the world? We say that we want our independence and when He gives it to us, we complain about the results.

We can't have it both ways, *"No one can serve two masters; for either he will hate the one and love the other, or else he will be loyal to the one and despise the other. You cannot serve God and mammon."* (Matt 6:24 NKJV) We can't say we want control of our lives and then want God to fix it for us all the time. He tells us how to live in His Word. If we choose to live that way, then blessings will follow. (Duet 28:2 NKJV) If we choose to not follow God and obey, then curses follow. (Deut 28:15 NKJV)

From the time in the garden, God has wanted to walk through life with us. We had it the way it was meant to be in the garden. The time in the Garden of Eden was like many people expect of God. But our brokenness and desire to have it our way broke that bond. God sent His only Son to restore that relationship.

This choice has been since creation started. The choice is ours. Here Joshua was letting the Israelites know whom he was going to serve, *"And if it seems evil to you to serve the LORD, choose for yourselves this day whom you will serve, whether the gods which your fathers served that were on the other side of the River, or the gods of the Amorites, in whose land you dwell. But as for me and my house, we will serve the LORD."* (Joshua 24:15 NKJV) Joshua challenged them to choose for themselves this day.

Pray that we choose wisely.

CHAPTER 3

GRACE AND TRUTH

"For the law was given through Moses, but grace and truth came through Jesus Christ."

(JOHN 1:17 NKJV)

Christianity is hard because there is a tension between grace and truth. Grace says that we are saved from all our sins by the blood of Jesus. We can do nothing to obtain salvation. It is a gift of God. Truth says that to be a disciple of Jesus Christ, we must surrender all and commit our life to Him.

If Christ has done everything for us, then why do we need to do anything? Salvation is a gift, *"For by grace you have been saved through faith, and that not of yourselves; it is the gift of God."* (Ephesians 2:8 NKJV) It is to be received freely. Yet, the cost to follow Jesus and be His disciple is high, *"Then Jesus said to His disciples, 'If anyone desires to come after Me, let him deny himself, and take up his cross, and follow Me.'"* (Matthew 16:24 NKJV) So, which is it?

And herein lies the tension: works should be a by-product of our faith. We cannot add anything to the finished work of Christ to secure our salvation. By accepting His offer, we are saved. If we try to add anything to His work, then that means His work was insufficient. His work on the cross was complete. Having Jesus work through us to accomplish works by faith is the answer.

Grace compels us to obedience. Once we fully understand the love and grace of the Lord Jesus Christ that He bestows on us, then the overwhelming desire to obey and follow Him is encountered. The only way to follow Jesus is through the grace of God and His love for us.

Grace leads to love. Love leads to obedience. Grace frees us to understand our need of a Savior. It gives us a desire to obey the spiritual and not the natural. Grace positions us to be able to recognize the spiritual battle that exists within us. It is our safety net. But just like a high-wire walker, we become less reliant on the net as our faith strengthens. We will always need the net until we are with the Lord and the sanctification process is complete. If we are in obedience, then He is our enabler. If we are in disobedience, then He is our disciplinarian and teacher. *"And having been perfected, He became the author of eternal salvation to all who obey Him."* (Hebrews 5:9 NKJV)

Grace versus the Law. Grace versus works. Faith, love, and works. Understanding these concepts and applying them to our life is difficult.

Jesus is Grace and Truth. He embodies both at the same time, *"For the law was given through Moses, but grace and truth came through Jesus Christ."* (John 1:17 NKJV) Many Christians try to work their way to heaven by abiding by the law. It doesn't work that way. Salvation is by the grace of God through faith in His Son. Not by the law or by works (Eph 2:8-9 NKJV) A prayer at the end of all of Paul's letters in the bible is, *"The grace of our Lord Jesus Christ be with you."* The one thing he consistently prays for all Christians is for us to have grace. The Bible ends with the same prayer, *"The grace of our Lord Jesus Christ be with you all. Amen."* (Rev 22:21 NKJV)

Grace enables us to have a relationship with God through His Son Jesus Christ. Grace is received by faith. Grace frees us to apply that faith in a daily, hourly, minute-to-minute walk with Jesus. It is the application of the faith, in which we freely receive grace, that we demonstrate our love for God. Only through the finished work of Jesus Christ on the cross can we even think about receiving grace and having a relationship with God the Father.

Thank God for His unlimited provision of grace to us. We seem to need more every day. Especially as the Spirit of God reveals more sin in our life. We are truly people who are Extra Grace Required (EGR). Grace, grace, and more grace: it seems that we can't get enough grace. How wonderful grace is to the woeful sinner such as we are, "*And of His fullness we have all received, and grace for grace.*" (John 1:16 NKJV) As we are working out our salvation, grace is a wonderful security net.

But we need to be careful that we do not fall into the trap of becoming enamored with grace. There are folks who wallow in grace. They never step out in faith. They hide behind the argument that it is all legalism. While the dangers of legalism are real, knowing the difference between obeying God and obeying man will provide the knowledge needed to follow Christ and avoid legalism. As Paul says, "*What shall we say then? Shall we continue in sin that grace may abound? Certainly not! How shall we who died to sin live any longer in it?*" (Romans 6:1–2 NKJV)

Christianity is hard because even though we are saved from our sins, there remains a consequence for our sins. It is by grace we are saved. Truth is the Lord has forgiven us of our sins; all our sins. It is a gift of God. Something that we can't earn. It can only be accepted. So, even though God has forgiven all of our sins, the truth is there still remains the consequence of sin (see chapter on Choice), "*For the wages of sin is death, but the gift of God is eternal life in Christ Jesus our Lord.*" (Romans 6:23 NKJV)

Christianity is hard because the discipline of God is real. Even though all of our sins have been forgiven by the grace of God, the truth is that God will discipline us as a child of God, "*My son, do not despise the chastening of the LORD, Nor be discouraged when you are rebuked by Him; For whom the LORD loves He chastens, And scourges every son whom He receives.*" (Hebrews 12:5b–6 NKJV) God disciplines us because He wants the best life for us. Just like earthly parents who discipline our children because we want the best for them, so does our heavenly Father. This is even more reason to embrace the grace of God and honor Him with our obedience. Pray for mercy when we know that discipline is coming.

Noah shows us the power of saving grace. When man needed it most,

Noah found grace, "*And the LORD was sorry that He had made man on the earth, and He was grieved in His heart. So the LORD said, 'I will destroy man whom I have created from the face of the earth, both man and beast, creeping thing and birds of the air, for I am sorry that I have made them.' But Noah found grace in the eyes of the LORD.*" (Genesis 6:6–8 NKJV) Noah saved humanity by grace from destruction.

Grace is being given a good thing that we don't deserve. Mercy is not being given a bad thing we do deserve. Mercy is saving us from judgment. Grace is giving us God's forgiveness. Truth is walking in God's love. It is accepting His word for our life and walking in it.

We need to provide to others the same grace that is given freely to us. We are not naturally people of grace. It is not in our nature to forgive people or give them something they haven't earned or deserve. It is only through and by the grace of God that we can do anything.

Grace is given to the humble. "*God resists the proud but gives grace to the humble.*" (James 4:6) The proud and arrogant will not receive grace. "*When pride comes, then comes shame; But with the humble is wisdom.*" (Proverbs 11:2 NKJV) Pride is the sin that caused Satan's fall from heaven (Is 14:12–14 NKJV) "*Humble yourselves in the sight of the Lord, and He will lift you up.*" (James 4:10 NKJV)

The book of Ephesians explains how grace and truth work together in a believer's life. Ephesians starts by describing who we are in Christ. We are chosen (1:4), loved (v4), a child of God (v5), accepted (v6), redeemed (v7), forgiven (v7), heirs (v11) and sealed with the Holy Spirit (v13 NKJV) This is our true identity, not the false lies of Satan. Paul then prays that God will give us the Spirit of wisdom and knowledge to know Jesus and these truths about us. These are all gifts from God, "*For by grace you have been saved through faith, and that not of yourselves; it is the gift of God, not of works, lest anyone should boast.*" (Ephesians 2:8–9 NKJV) He has created all of this for us so that we can perform good works for Him. (Eph 2:10 NKJV) We are Christ's workmanship.

The rest of the book of Ephesians "walks" us through how to live out of the grace we received to bring glory to our Lord. Paul beseeches us to "*walk worthy of the calling.*" (Eph 4:1 NKJV) He warns us to not "*walk as the rest of the gentiles walk.*" (4:17) Our new identity should compel us to good works. We should walk in the example of Christ, "*Walk in love as Christ has loved us and given Himself for us*" (5:1). We should "*walk as children of the Light*" demonstrating the fruits of the Spirit (5:8). Then understanding the will of the Lord, we should "*walk circumspectly, not as fools but as wise*" (5:15). The truth is that we are a new creature in Christ. Use the gifts and talents that God has given us for His glory, by His grace.

Christianity is hard because in America, truth is what we make it. As an example, there is someone who is suing because he wants to be a different age. He wants to be twenty years younger. Age is defined by how long we have been on this earth alive. There is no changing that truth. We used to say that the line between right and wrong is blurred. It appears to not exist for many people. Jesus defines the truth for all. Whether they choose to believe it or not doesn't make it any less the truth. And this makes it very difficult for some people to accept the truth that Jesus is the Son of God.

This is a ploy of Satan: that is to have us question what is truth, "*The coming of the lawless one is according to the working of Satan, with all power, signs, and lying wonders, and with all unrighteous deception among those who perish, because they did not receive the love of the truth, that they might be saved. And for this reason, God will send them strong delusion, that they should believe the lie, that they all may be condemned who did not believe the truth but had pleasure in unrighteousness.*" (2 Thes 2:9–12 NKJV) By questioning the truth, Satan pulls us away from God. That is his ultimate game: have us question the truth and make poor choices by believing his lies.

There are some who are "*always learning and never able to come to the knowledge of the truth.*" (2 Timothy 3:7 NKJV) They study and learn because they want to know. The only way to know the truth is to believe and act on that belief. There are others who resist the truth, "*so do these also resist the truth: men of corrupt minds, disapproved concerning the faith.*" (2 Timothy 3:8 NKJV) They don't want to accept that the Gospel is true. They will fight themselves and others rather than believe.

There is a way to prove the truth, "*And do not be conformed to this world, but be transformed by the renewing of your mind, that you may prove what is that good and acceptable and perfect will of God.*" (Romans 12:2 NKJV) Once we find the good and acceptable will of God, we have found the truth (See chapter on Gods will).

Truth is the Word of God, "*Sanctify them by Your truth. Your word is truth.*" (John 17:17 NKJV) And for the truth to be in us, we must obey the Word, "*He who says, 'I know Him,' and does not keep His commandments, is a liar, and the truth is not in him.*" (1 John 2:4 NKJV) So, when people argue between grace and truth, they argue about obeying the Word of God or living in God's grace. Let this be the testimony of our faith journey, that by the grace of Lord Jesus Christ we walk in the truth. "*For I rejoiced greatly when brethren came and testified of the truth that is in you, just as you walk in the truth. I have no greater joy than to hear that my children walk in truth.*" (3 John 1:3–4 NKJV) Our actions should reflect our faith and our belief in the truth, "*My little children, let us not love in word or in tongue, but in deed and in truth. And by this we know that we are of the truth and shall assure our hearts before Him.*" (1 John 3:18–19 NKJV)

Read God's word every day. Place the truth, God's Word, in our heart. Use the Word of God to fend off Satan, "*The word is powerful and sharper than any two-edged sword.*" (Heb 4:12 NKJV) The Spirit convicts us of the truth and guides us into making good decisions if we will yield to Him, "*However, when He, the Spirit of truth, has come, He will guide you into all truth.*" (John 16:13a NKJV) Besides the Word of God (truth) to help us, God has given us the Spirit, "*And I will pray the Father, and He will give you another Helper, that He may abide with you forever—the Spirit of truth, whom the world cannot receive, because it neither sees Him nor knows Him; but you know Him, for He dwells with you and will be in you.*" (John 14:16–17 NKJV) And furthermore, the world will not receive the Spirit because they do not realize He exists. They can't see Him nor know Him because they don't believe. They are not willing to accept that Jesus is the Lord, and therefore they do not receive the Holy Spirit.

The Bible provides another example of an opportunity to believe. At the cross, a soldier pierces the side of Jesus to see if He is dead. Blood and water come out of Jesus which fulfills prophesy. When someone testifies of the truth, will we believe them? *"And he who has seen has testified, and his testimony is true; and he knows that he is telling the truth, so that you may believe."* (John 19:35 NKJV) When we hear the truth, will we believe it? Only by the grace of God can we believe.

Worshipping God requires that we worship Him in spirit and truth, *"God is Spirit, and those who worship Him must worship in spirit and truth."* (John 4:24 NKJV) We must be sincere in our worship. We can't halve it. Worshipping God takes all our heart, mind, and soul. He wants us to be all in. God is a holy and just God. It is part of the sanctification process. For us to be conformed into His likeness. Jesus provides access to the Father, *"Jesus said to him, 'I am the way, the truth, and the life. No one comes to the Father except through Me.'"* (John 14:6 NKJV)

Please don't underestimate the holiness of God and His willingness to let us be us. God doesn't like unrighteousness and will execute justice against those who suppress the truth, *"For the wrath of God is revealed from heaven against all ungodliness and unrighteousness of men, who suppress the truth in unrighteousness."* (Romans 1:18 NKJV) God will also let us be us in all our unrighteousness, *"Therefore God also gave them up to uncleanness, in the lusts of their hearts, to dishonor their bodies among themselves, who exchanged the truth of God for the lie, and worshiped and served the creature rather than the Creator, who is blessed forever."* (Romans 1:24–25 NKJV) Some folks will believe the lie. Because God gives us the choice, He will let them live in their lie.

Jesus provided a way for us to escape all this unrighteousness and judgment. Then Jesus said to those who believed Him, *"If you abide in My word, you are My disciples indeed. And you shall know the truth, and the truth shall make you free."* (John 8:31–32 NKJV) The truth frees us from the body of sin to live a life dedicated to the Lord. We are servants to the Lord, yet we are free. It is a contradiction that only can be believed and experienced. If we try to understand it without believing, we will never come to know the truth.

In Luke, Jesus tells us a story about the rich man and Lazarus. Lazarus is sitting in heaven and the rich man is being tormented in Hades. The rich man begs Abraham to go and warn his brothers of this place called Hades. The ending dialogue goes like this, "*Then he said, 'I beg you therefore, father, that you would send him to my father's house, for I have five brothers, that he may testify to them, lest they also come to this place of torment.' Abraham said to him, 'They have Moses and the prophets; let them hear them.' And he said, 'No, father Abraham; but if one goes to them from the dead, they will repent.' But he said to him, 'If they do not hear Moses and the prophets, neither will they be persuaded though one rise from the dead.'*" (Luke 16:27–31 NKJV) Some just won't believe. It is sad.

There will be a judgment for those who choose poorly, "*But we know that the judgment of God is according to truth against those who practice such things.*" (Romans 2:2 NKJV) Even though God today lets them live in their ignorance and rebellion, He will one day bring judgment on them. And for us who say that God shouldn't let that happen, how else would He know if we truly love Him? We have a choice. This story shows that even if someone comes from the dead, some people still won't believe.

God has provided a way for all to know, "*For since the creation of the world His invisible attributes are clearly seen, being understood by the things that are made, even His eternal power and Godhead, so that they are without excuse, because, although they knew God, they did not glorify Him as God, nor were thankful, but became futile in their thoughts, and their foolish hearts were darkened.*" (Romans 1:20-21 NKJV) He has set it in their heart to know. But because people have let their hearts be hardened and darkened, they have kept themselves from believing the truth. The Spirit of God draws us to God. He works on our hearts to make us aware of God and our need of Him. "*Now we have received, not the spirit of the world, but the Spirit who is from God, that we might know the things that have been freely given to us by God.*" (1 Cor 2:12 NKJV) People are without an excuse.

There is a conundrum in the Christian faith. On the one hand,

Salvation is a gift of God, "*For by grace you have been saved through faith, and that not of yourselves; it is the gift of God.*" (Ephesians 2:8 NKJV) It is to be received freely. We can do nothing to earn it. God couldn't have made it easier. Christ did everything for us. This is the truth of God.

On the other hand, to be a disciple of Christ and follow him, we are to suffer, deny ourselves, and pick up our cross. Jesus commands us to follow Him, "*And he who does not take his cross and follow after Me is not worthy of Me.*" (Matthew 10:38 NKJV) To follow Jesus and be His disciple takes everything including our life. Then Jesus said to His disciples, "*If anyone desires to come after Me, let him deny himself, and take up his cross, and follow Me. For whoever desires to save his life will lose it, but whoever loses his life for My sake will find it.*" (Matthew 16:24–25 NKJV) This is a truth of God.

The truth is that God loves us and "*desires all men to be saved and to come to the knowledge of the truth.*" (1 Timothy 2:4 NKJV) He has shown them the truth. People have enough now to believe. After God has done many things for us to know, He is saying, "*And then they shall know I am the Lord.*" (Ezekiel 16:62 NKJV) And marvels when we don't believe.

In Galatians, Paul is talking to the Galatians about the Jewish practice of circumcision. Circumcision was given to the Jewish people to protect them at a time when it was necessary to prevent infection. When we as a people place this "work" on individuals as part of their salvation or to increase their relationship with Christ, then it is legalism. Jesus + Nothing = Everything. We cannot add anything to the finished work of Jesus Christ at the cross. He saved us completely. Paul concludes this section with "*For in Christ Jesus neither circumcision nor uncircumcision avails anything, but faith working through love.*" (Gal 5:6 NKJV)

Faith working through Love. How perfect of a statement to epitomize the walk of a disciple. Grace enables that truth. It is only by the grace of God that we can walk in the truth.

"*I have no greater joy than to hear that my children walk in truth.*" (3 John 1:4 NKJV)

CHAPTER 4

KNOWING GOD

"Then you shall know that I am Lord."

(EZEKIEL 16:62B NKJV)

C hristianity is hard because we are asked to know God that we can't physically see or hear. God wants us to know Him as Lord. He is doing many things in our life to let us know He is Lord. Whether we recognize or realize it doesn't mean it isn't so.

God has provided many ways for us to know Him. He has sent His Son to pay for our sins and restore the relationship. He has torn the veil providing access to Him. He has provided the Holy Spirit to live within us to teach us, guide us, and help us in our faith journey. He has given us the world that reveal His attributes to know Him, *"For since the creation of the world His invisible attributes are clearly seen, being understood by the things that are made, even His eternal power and Godhead, so that they are without excuse."* (Romans 1:20 NKJV) We are without excuse to know God.

God continues to show His work. He works in people's live to reveal Himself to them. God wanted to show them who He is and that He is real. He still wants to show us. Jesus is working in our life to let us know that He is the Lord. Sixty-nine times, in Ezekiel, after doing something to get the attention of His people, the Lord states, "*Then they shall know I am Lord.*" (Ezekiel 16:62b NKJV) The Lord is trying to get our attention.

After reading through Ezekiel, we must wonder what God is doing in our life to let us know that He is Lord. How many times did He do something to get our attention? To steer us clear of some danger. To reveal a better way. How many times did we stubbornly refuse to acknowledge that it was God? What is God doing in our life that will let us know that He wants to have a relationship with us? God is trying to get our attention so we can be in a relationship with Him.

How do we know that God exists? Because we believe. We can sense Him. His presence. His Love. We can feel apart from God when we have sin in our life. We have been disciplined and He continually disciplines us as a child of God, "*For whom the LORD loves He chastens, and scourges every son whom He receives.*" (Hebrews 12:6 NKJV) He has blessed and continues to bless our families. He has answered and continues to answer our prayers (not always the way we expected). We can see the results of His actions. We can talk to Him daily. This is all done through faith.

Christianity is hard because to know God, we must be in the Spirit. How can the demons know Him and we have so much trouble? Jesus is casting out demons and He wouldn't let them talk because they knew Him, "*Then He healed many who were sick with various diseases and cast out many demons; and He did not allow the demons to speak, because they knew Him.*" (Mark 1:34 NKJV) If they knew Him, why wouldn't they repent? It must be pride. They know Him because they are living in the Spirit world vice the earthly world. To know God, we must know Him in the Spirit.

Christianity is hard because the Spirit of God is a mystery to most of us. God has given us the Spirit to dwell inside of us to help us to understand God. To know God is to know the Spirit of God, because God is Spirit. God commands us to worship Him in the Spirit. "*But the hour is coming, and now is, when the true worshipers will worship the Father in spirit and truth; for the Father is seeking such to worship Him. God is Spirit, and those who worship Him must worship in spirit and truth.*" (John

4:23–24 NKJV) We must acknowledge His presence and yield to Him to gain the understanding. This is one of the greatest mysteries of God.

To gain access to the Spirit's power and knowledge, we must yield to Him and seek His guidance. It takes faith. It takes knowledge that this is true. But through practice, the believer becomes more confident or knowledgeable that this is truth. This is what Luke means when he says, *"Nor will they say, 'See here!' or 'See there!' For indeed, the kingdom of God is within you."* (Luke 17:20–21 NKJV) To truly know God, we must believe, worship, and know in the Spirit. We must trust that the Spirit will tell us. Without Him, we are lost and unknowing.

Christianity is hard because we try to find knowledge in other places and people than from God. All understanding comes from God, *"And we know that the Son of God has come and has given us an understanding, that we may know Him who is true; and we are in Him who is true, in His Son Jesus Christ. This is the true God and eternal life."* (1 John:20 NKJV) And why has God given us understanding? It is to know Him.

God provides the Bible to us to gain knowledge. The scriptures say that the first thing we should know is that the Bible is the Word of God, *"Knowing this first, that no prophecy of Scripture is of any private ᵉinterpretation, for prophecy never came by the will of man, but holy men of God spoke as they were moved by the Holy Spirit."* (2 Pet 1:20–21 NKJV) If we don't believe that the Bible is the Word of God, then it is a nonstarter for obtaining knowledge and wisdom. And we must believe the whole Bible is the Word of God. We can't just believe that parts of the Bible are true and not the whole book. It is either all or nothing. This frees us up to start to really understand the power of the Word of God.

Peter gives us instruction and a warning on how to handle the knowledge of God through the scriptures. He warns us that some things are hard to understand, and that other people will twist them to their own destruction, *"In which are some things hard to understand, which untaught and unstable people twist to their own destruction, as they do also the rest of the Scriptures."* (2 Peter 3:16b NKJV) Next, Peter tells us to grow in the knowledge of the Lord, not in knowledge of other things. We should grow in knowing the Lord, which starts with the Word of God. "*You therefore, beloved, since you know this beforehand, beware lest you also fall from your own steadfastness, being led away with the error of the wicked; but grow in the grace and knowledge of our Lord and Savior Jesus Chris.*" (2 Peter 3:17–18 NKJV)

Knowledge will only take us so far. If we don't act on the knowledge and follow Jesus by doing His will, then Jesus will say this to us, "*I will declare to them, 'I never knew you; depart from Me, you who practice lawlessness!*'" (Matt 7:23 NKJV) A deeper look into this passage reveals that for the Lord to know us requires that we do His will, "*Not everyone who says to Me, 'Lord, Lord,' shall enter the kingdom of heaven, but he who does the will of My Father in heaven.*" (Matt 7:21 NKJV) There should be fruit from our faith, "*Therefore by their fruits you will know them.*" (Matt 7:20 NKJV) Knowledge ought to be sought after, but the application of that knowledge ought to glorify God.

Be careful if we profess to know God and our works say otherwise. We should watch what people do and not what they say. Because what people do is what is in their hearts. People can say anything, but when they do it, then we know they mean it. When someone backs up what they say with actions, it provides certain validity to their statements. It validates their faith. It goes to show what is in their heart, "*They profess to know God, but in works they deny Him, being abominable, disobedient, and disqualified for every good work.*" (Titus 1:16 NKJV)

Christianity is hard because we are thick. Mark 8:14–21 NKJV highlights the unbelief that occurs in human beings. The twelve apostles realize they don't have enough bread to feed themselves. This is after seeing the two miracles of feeding thousands with seven fish one time and five another time. Jesus at this point marvels, "*How is it you do not understand?*" (Mark 8:21 NKJV) What is it going to take for us to grasp the love that the Lord wants to bestow on us? It is difficult. If faith were easy, then everyone would have it. That is the very nature of faith. We must believe in something we can't touch or see physically. We believe that we can 'see'

God, Jesus, and the Holy Spirit in our lives every day. We must look with a believing heart.

Christianity is hard because knowledge is a gift from God and therefore can be given or taken at any time, *"that the God of our Lord Jesus Christ, the Father of glory, may give to you the spirit of wisdom and revelation in the knowledge of Him, the eyes of your understanding being enlightened; that you may know what is the hope of His calling, what are the riches of the glory of His inheritance in the saints."* (Eph 1:17–18 NKJV) Here the Lord "may give" knowledge and I believe He can also take it away depending on our Spirit and motivation for the use. It also depends on whether He will be glorified in the use of knowledge.

God can hide knowledge from us, *"In that hour Jesus rejoiced in the Spirit and said, 'I thank You, Father, Lord of heaven and earth, that You have hidden these things from the wise and prudent and revealed them to babes. Even so, Father, for so it seemed good in Your sight.'"* (Luke 10:21 NKJV) Jesus tells the disciples about the things which must happen in Jerusalem. He tells them about His death. *"But they understood none of these things; this saying was hidden from them, and they did not know the things which were spoken."* (Luke 18:34 NKJV) So, God is the source of all wisdom. He can take it or give it at any time. We must acknowledge this fact if we are truly to become wise. All knowledge comes from God, *"And He opened their understanding, that they might comprehend the Scriptures."* (Luke 24:45 NKJV)

Christianity is hard because we need a new heart to understand the hidden things of God, *"Then I will give them a heart to know Me, that I am the LORD; and they shall be My people, and I will be their God, for they shall return to Me with their whole heart."* (Jeremiah 24:7 NKJV) We receive a new heart when we accept Jesus as our Lord and Savior. Our old heart won't see the glory of God. It takes a change of heart to see the evidence of faith. Because we have rejected God, He doesn't owe us anything. It takes the grace of God to open our eyes.

Christianity is hard because it takes work. We need to meditate on God's Word day and night. *"This Book of the Law shall not depart from your mouth, but you shall meditate in it day and night, that you may* *observe to do according to all that is written in it. For then you will make* *your way prosperous, and then you will have good success."* (Joshua 1:8 NKJV) The Holy Spirit is there to help us understand what we are reading in the Bible. We should study God's Word every day. Then the Word of God will be in our hearts when we need it to fight our spiritual battles.

Jesus Christ's work on the cross tore the veil that was used to protect the Holy of Holies. The veil being split in two provides access to God through Jesus Christ. The veil kept the Israelites from entering the Holy of Holies. This was the sacred area of the temple where only the high priest could enter once a year to atone for the sins of the nation of Israel, *"The* *veil shall be a divider for you between the holy place and the Most Holy."* (Exodus 26:33 NKJV) When Jesus died for our sins, the veil was torn, *"Then the veil of the temple was torn in two from top to bottom."* (Mark 15:38 NKJV) This provides us direct and daily access to God through the work of Christ. *"Therefore, brethren, having boldness to enter the Holiest* *by the blood of Jesus, by a new and living way which He consecrated for us,* *through the veil, that is, His flesh, and having a High Priest over the house* *of God."* (Hebrews 10:19–21 NKJV) Jesus Christ provided us a way to restore the relationship with the Father, *"Nevertheless when one turns to* *the Lord, the veil is taken away. Now the Lord is the Spirit; and where the* *Spirit of the Lord is, there is liberty."* (2 Cor 3:16–17 NKJV)

Christianity is hard because we need to humble ourselves daily. Just when we think we know the Lord, be careful. Knowledge can make us conceited and then we think we are someone special. There is a warning, *"Now concerning things offered to idols: We know that we all have knowl-* *edge. Knowledge puffs up, but love edifies. And if anyone thinks that he* *knows anything, he knows nothing yet as he ought to know. But if anyone* *loves God, this one is known by Him."* (1 Cor 8:1–3 NKJV) We should strive to know God and seek Him with all our heart, mind, and soul. We can never fully know God until the time has come.

If we are doing something just to glorify ourselves or be puffed up, then the Spirit will not reveal the knowledge to us. So we always must be careful to yield to the Spirit in everything and He will provide the answer, "*Now when they bring you to the synagogues and magistrates and authorities, do not worry about how or what you should answer, or what you should say. For the Holy Spirit will teach you in that very hour what you ought to say.*" (Luke 12:11–12 NKJV)

Christianity is hard because religion gets in the way. God wants us to come to Him as little children, not as scholarly know-it-alls. Some people fight over different Christian theories. Premillennial and post millennial are two that seem to always be a topic of conversation. People are struggling to know. If we are saved, then it really doesn't matter. God is going to take care of us. Do we believe it?

They do this in hope of coming closer to God and knowing Him. They argue over who is right instead of looking to God. They bring other things to the simple plan of God. They lose the real importance of God's plan. It is simple. They struggle to outwit each other. A key to knowing God is to debase ourselves. The reality is that we know nothing without Him. He is the source of all knowledge and wisdom. Stay true to God and it won't matter whether the premillennial or post millennial happens.

Christianity is hard because we must be willing to give up our old selves and start a new life. God heals a blind man so that folks will know that He is Lord, "*Jesus answered, 'Neither this man nor his parents sinned, but that the works of God should be revealed in him.'*" (John 9:3 NKJV) The Pharisees did not believe because they had hardened their hearts and feared losing their lives as they knew it. The struggle with what they knew to be true and what was true. They need to be willing to let go of their lives to be able to believe. They didn't want to believe that a man who was blind could be healed. The sinner began to teach the Pharisees. They were indignant because who was this blind man to teach them? They trusted in all their studies. Faith is a simple process and to know the Lord takes a simple heart and faith. Faith is too simple for people who want to know. The Pharisees were not open to the truth. They scared the Jews into not saying anything publicly about Jesus. We must be willing to lose our life to be able to hear the truth. John the Baptist was willing to diminish so that

Jesus could increase. (John 3:30 NKJV) This is the attitude that we must obtain. We cannot cling to our lives when it comes to hearing the Word of God and obeying.

To know God, we must believe in heavenly things. We must know Him in the Spirit and know the Spirit. *"Most assuredly, I say to you, we speak what we know and testify what we have seen, and you do not receive Our witness. If I have told you earthly things and you do not believe, how will you believe if I tell you heavenly things?"* (John 3:11–12 NKJV) If we don't understand in earthly terms, we will have trouble believing in heavenly terms. Our minds try to comprehend everything in what we know, earthly things. As we let go to the knowledge of the Spirit, we start to understand things in heavenly terms. An example of this is time. God is above time. He is always present in any time. So when we are impatient, to God it just the blink of an eye. One day is like a thousand to Him, *"But, beloved, do not forget this one thing, that with the Lord one day is as a thousand years, and a thousand years as one day."* (2 Peter 3:8 NKJV)

Christianity is hard because people struggle to understand the depths of His love and grace for us. If we would only believe, then the door would be open to us. An example is like winning the lottery. Most people don't understand the amount of money they are about to receive from winning the lottery because they have never experienced it. When people dream about winning the $300M lottery, they describe buying a house or paying off their debt. Okay, what is the plan for the other $299M? It is the same with the grace and love of God. People don't understand the amount of grace and love that God wants to bestow on them. God warns us about a hardened heart that keeps us from believing, *"Beware, brethren, lest there be in any of you an evil heart of unbelief in departing from the living God; but exhort one another daily, while it is called today, lest any of you be hardened through the deceitfulness of sin."* (Hebrews 3:12–13 NKJV)

Throughout the book of Daniel, Daniel interprets mysteries, dreams, and writings that no one else could interpret. These mysteries were made known to Daniel because he sought God with all his heart. In verse 1:8, it says, *"Daniel purposed in his heart that he would not defile himself with the* portion of the king's delicacies." (Dan 1:8 NKJV) He wanted to stay true to God. And for that belief, God gave Daniel and his three fellow servants *"knowledge and skill in all literature and wisdom; and Daniel had understanding in all visions and dreams."* (Dan 1:17 NKJV) Seek God with all your heart, mind, and soul, *"You will seek the LORD your God, and you will find Him if you seek Him with all your heart and with all your soul."* (Deut. 4:29 NKJV)

Knowledge of Jesus Christ is so important that the apostle Paul writes that he counts everything else as trash in comparison to knowing Jesus, *"Indeed I also count all things loss for the excellence of the knowledge of Christ Jesus my Lord, for whom I have suffered the loss of all things, and count them as rubbish, that I may gain Christ."* (Philippians 3:8 NKJV)

One day we will all know that Jesus is Lord because *"at the name of Jesus every knee should bow, of those in heaven, and of those on earth, and of those under the earth, and that every tongue should confess that Jesus Christ is Lord, to the glory of God the Father."* (Philippians 2:10–11 NKJV) But if we wait until this moment, it will be too late. (look at the chapter on Choice)

Christianity is hard because we don't always recognize when God is trying to get our attention. Here are some examples of God trying to get people's attention: God blinds Paul on the Damascus road for three days to let Him know He has a plan for his life; God has the rooster crow three times for Peter to realize God wants him to know Him as Lord and be the leader of His church; Moses and the burning bush; Daniel and the lion's den; God puts Jonah in the belly of a fish for three days to get Him to know; and God sends the nation of Israel to captivity to know that He is Lord.

What is God doing in our life to get our attention? To let us know that He is Lord. Jesus prays to Father for us, *"And this is eternal life, that they may know You, the only true God, and Jesus Christ whom You have sent."* (John 17:3 NKJV)

Pray that we realize that Jesus is working in our life so that we will know that He is Lord.

CHAPTER 5

LOVING GOD

"Love the Lord your God with all your heart, mind and soul."

(LUKE 10:27 NKJV)

C hristianity is hard because our minds have difficulty grasping all the love, power and awesomeness of God. God is Love. God is Spirit. God is eternal. God is just. God wants to be our God and for us to be His people. *"As God has said: 'I will dwell in them And walk among them. I will be their God, And they shall be My people.'"* (2 Corinthians 6:16b, Lev 26:12, Jer 31:33, and Zech 8:8 NKJV) God created us to be in relationship with Him. Knowing God is what matters. All else pales in comparison. We need to know who God is to be able to love Him. Jesus prays for us that we may know that eternal life is knowing God, *"And this is eternal life, that they may know You, the only true God, and Jesus Christ whom You have sent."* (John 17:3 NKJV)

Christianity is hard because knowing God is revealed through the Trinity of God. God the Father, God the Son, and God the Holy Spirit make up the Trinity of God. Each person of the Trinity relates to us differently, *"The grace of the Lord Jesus Christ, and the love of God, and the communion of the Holy Spirit be with you all."* (2 Corinthians 13:14 NKJV) Each person of the Trinity plays a part in our faith journey. How to relate to each one is an exercise in faith. The Trinity causes many to not believe because it is hard to understand or comprehend. As we learn to relate to each member of the Trinity, then the Trinity itself makes sense.

We cannot know God using worldly knowledge and wisdom. It is useless without faith in God, *"For since, in the wisdom of God, the world through wisdom did not know God, it pleased God through the foolishness of the message preached to save those who believe."* (1 Corinthians 1:21 NKJV) We must submit to God and believe that He is to know Him.

God desires *"that all men to be saved and come to the knowledge of Jesus Christ."* (1Tim 2:4 NKJV) Our relationship to God was broken after the fall in the Garden of Eden. Only through His finished work on the cross can we have a relationship with the Father. The truth is Jesus wants us to know Him as Lord. That is the whole point of the gospel. That is to restore the relationship that was lost in the garden.

Christianity is hard because sin damages the relationship and separates us from God. He loves us so much that He doesn't want these things to damage the relationship, but we do them anyway. (Isaiah 59:2, Psalm 66:18).

Christianity is hard because God is holy. God is holy and requires justice for sin. That means He is just and will impart justice for those who do not choose Jesus as their Lord, *"And these will go away into everlasting punishment, but the righteous into eternal life."* (Matthew 25:46 NKJV) *"These"* refers to those who have not accepted Jesus as their Savior.

God wants us to be holy, *"For this is the will of God, your sanctification."* (1 Thessalonians 4:3a NKJV) Positionally, we are holy once we accept Jesus as our Savior, *"By that will we have been sanctified through the offering of the body of Jesus Christ once for all."* (Hebrews 10:10 NKJV) *"By that will"* refers to God's will, which Jesus followed to the cross for us. Until the time is complete, we are in the process of sanctification. Sanctification is the process of making us holy. God accomplishes this in us through our sanctification, *"For God did not call us to uncleanness, but in holiness."* (1 Thessalonians 4:7 NKJV)

Christianity is hard because God is just. He will execute justice on sin and those that aren't found in the book of life. This is hard to accept because He created us. He could have created us to love Him instead of the ability to choose to love Him. It is hard to love a God who will execute justice on many of our loved ones. He has charged us with changing their minds and making disciples. Thank God who sent His Son, Jesus, to the earth to show us the way. This should persuade us to make sure they are aware of the consequences of their decision.

Why do so many have to go to hell? Can't we save them all? This is a rather long passage but covers the need for people to acknowledge and respond God's call. Some of us are just plain stubborn, "*So it was that the beggar died, and was carried by the angels to Abraham's bosom. The rich man also died and was buried. And being in torments in Hades, he lifted up his eyes and saw Abraham afar off, and Lazarus in his bosom. Then he cried and said, 'Father Abraham, have mercy on me, and send Lazarus that he may dip the tip of his finger in water and cool my tongue; for I am tormented in this flame.' But Abraham said, 'Son, remember that in your lifetime you received your good things, and likewise Lazarus evil things; but now he is comforted and you are tormented. And besides all this, between us and you there is a great gulf fixed, so that those who want to pass from here to you cannot, nor can those from there pass to us.' Then he said, 'I beg you therefore, father, that you would send him to my father's house, for I have five brothers, that he may testify to them, lest they also come to this place of torment.' Abraham said to him, 'They have Moses and the prophets; let them hear them.' And he said, 'No, father Abraham; but if one goes to them from the dead, they will repent.' But he said to him, 'If they do not hear Moses and the prophets, neither will they be persuaded though one rise from the dead.*" (Luke 16:22–31 NKJV)

Hell is real. People aren't willing to accept that truth. It is ironic that even after Jesus rose from the dead, there were many in that day who still didn't believe. So, the last statement (Luke 16:31) is prophetic and sadly true. There is no other explanation as to why so many don't drop everything and follow God. Doesn't it frustrate us that folks don't get it? If so, then pray that people will understand the clue God has already given us.

Christianity is hard because our love pales in comparison to God's love. When we lie to someone we love, it hurts them and us. It hurts to the point that we want to make it right, immediately, if we truly love them. That is the way it should be when we sin against God. Sin is against God and God alone. As David states, *"Against You, You only, have I sinned, And done this evil in Your sight."* (Psalm 51:4a NKJV) The Holy Spirit will let us know that we have sinned if we are yielded to Him and have a softened heart. He will reveal more and more sin in our life. As He purges, and we let Him, the sin from our life, we will feel the freedom that John describes, *"Therefore if the Son makes you free, you shall be free indeed."* (John 8:36 NKJV) This is the sanctification process. This is a test of the level of relationship and love for God in our life. Does it hurt us when we sin against God?

God continues to pursue us and work in our lives even when we are far from Him. We must be paying attention to notice the works of God in our life. We miss chances to understand that God is working in our life because we aren't looking for it. In the verse below, someone points out in exclamation to look. Wouldn't it be nice to have someone exclaim, "Look!" every time God is working in our life? It would be happening more than most people think. In the book of Daniel, King Nebuchadnezzar in amazement says, *"Look!" he answered, "I see four men loose, walking in the midst of the fire; and they are not hurt, and the form of the fourth is like the Son of God."* (Daniel 3:25 NKJV)

Christianity is hard because God is going to do what God is going to do. In this verse, God tells Moses, *"I will have mercy on whomever I will have mercy, and I will have compassion on whomever I will have compassion."* (Romans 9:15 NKJV) God is sovereign. That is difficult for some people to accept. In our relationship with Him, we must accept that God is going to do what God wants to do. It may be to our benefit and it may not. We must stay true to God because He is sovereign and to do anything else is foolishness. Why would we go against the maker of the universe? We are in His world, not the other way around.

Christianity is hard because our ways are not God's ways. Some of this faith journey doesn't make any sense. If God is good, then why does He allow such evil in this world? Why do innocent children die? Why is evil present? We realize that as humans, we have sinned and failed God, but why is the penalty so severe? We have a choice (see the chapter on Choice) We once had it exactly the way that most expect it to be now. That was in the Garden of Eden. We as a people chose to seek the knowledge of good and evil. And since that fall, we now know evil. Jesus came to restore that relationship.

Christianity is hard because we are to serve out of love and not fear. The best way to serve the Lord is because we love Him. Jesus said, "*If you love Me, keep My commandments.*" (John 14:15 NKJV) If we don't serve out of love, then we will end up despising the work of the Lord. If we serve out of fear, then our motive is based on staying out of trouble and our effort is unsustainable.

People either love the Lord or fear Him, or both. They serve or obey the Lord through either love or fear. We are commanded to love the Lord with all our heart, mind, and soul. So we should obey the Lord through love, but sometimes we obey through fear. Once we choose to love God and walk by faith, then fear becomes nonexistent to us. This is very hard to understand, but there is a way to know: when the peace of God is on us is when we are trusting in the Lord completely. We can either serve Him through fear or through love. When we serve Him through love, fear goes away, "*There is no fear in love; but perfect love casts out fear, because fear involves torment. But he who fears has not been made perfect in love.*" (1 John 4:18 NKJV)

Jude is talking about saving people with the Word of God. He stresses, "*On some have compassion, making a distinction, but others save with fear….*" (Jude 22–23 NKJV) This shows the two approaches to serving and loving God. We will either love Him or fear Him.

Paul also understood the difference between serving through love or fear. Paul asks the Corinthian church how should he come, in love or with a whip? "*What do you want? Shall I come to you with a rod, or in love and a spirit of gentleness?*" (1 Cor 3:21 NKJV)

Christianity is hard because there is a consequence to not loving God. For those who choose not to love God and receive the truth, condemnation will follow, and they will end up fearing the Lord, "*with all unrighteous deception among those who perish, because they did not receive the love of the truth, that they might be saved. And for this reason God will send them strong delusion, that they should believe the lie, that they all may be condemned who did not believe the truth but had pleasure in unrighteousness.*" (2 Thes 2:10–12 NKJV) And the result of this unbelief and denial of God is, "*Then I saw another angel flying in the midst of heaven, having the everlasting gospel to preach to those who dwell on the earth— to every nation, tribe, tongue, and people—saying with a loud voice, 'Fear God and give glory to Him, for the hour of His judgment has come.'*" (Rev 14:6,7 NKJV) Look at the difference in the gospel messages. Here when the judgment has come the message is "Fear God." Compare this with the gospel message at the beginning of Jesus' ministry, "*The time is fulfilled, and the kingdom of God is at hand. Repent, and believe in the gospel.*" (Mark 1:15 NKJV)

Christianity is hard because we miss out on opportunities to glorify Jesus, "*Therefore, since a promise remains of entering His rest, let us fear lest any of you seem to have come short of it.*" (Heb 4:1 NKJV) This doesn't mean that we must work at it or that it comes by works. It means that we must believe, completely, "*So we see that they could not enter in because of unbelief.*" (Hebrews 3:19 NKJV) Not believe some today or some tomorrow, or when we are in trouble, but all the time. Does our relationship reflect that belief? It is a great honor to be used of God.

There is a fear that the person we share the Gospel with wouldn't ever hear that word or come to know Christ if we don't say the right thing or do the right action. Their salvation isn't up to us and God can still accomplish His will without us. That is for sure. Although it is an honor to be used by God to reach our loved ones.

Christianity is hard because we continue to fail God, or at least think we are failing Him. Another one that hurts is when we can glorify God and fail to act. When we look back at the day and realize that we had a chance and failed, we repent and ask the Lord to forgive us. These opportunities can be as easy as saying a word to another person. Or sharing our heart. Or forgiving someone. It is just a demonstration of God's love to someone else. God is bigger than any of our failings. Remember that it is a loving relationship.

It would be better to serve the Lord in love than fear, but we will acknowledge that he exists. As it is stated inPhil 2:9–11 NKJV, "*Therefore God also has highly exalted Him and given Him the name which is above every name, that at the name of Jesus every knee should bow, of those in heaven, and of those on earth, and of those under the earth, and that every tongue should confess that Jesus Christ is Lord, to the glory of God the Father.*" That is every knee. Everyone will confess that Jesus Christ is Lord! Notice what Paul writes next: he exhorts us to work out our salvation with fear and trembling. Once we work out our salvation, we will love the Lord and no longer fear Him. This is the level of sanctification to attain. We ought to let the Lord work on us to attain the level that Paul states, "*Be anxious for nothing, but in everything by prayer and supplication, with thanksgiving, let your requests be made known to God; and the peace of God, which surpasses all understanding, will guard your hearts and minds through Christ Jesus.*" (Phil 4:6-7 NKJV) And again, later in the chapter, "*Not that I speak in regard to need, for I have learned in whatever state I am, to be content.*" (Phil 4:11 NKJV) That is the state to be in: total reliance on God. When we are in this state, there is nothing to fear.

The life of a disciple is one in which we walk in close relationship with Christ. Jesus' followers were always with Him. A disciple is a dedicated follower. A disciple learns from His master. He wants us to be like Him. Being in a relationship with Jesus is easy and difficult at the same time. It is full of grace and truth at the same time. Jesus and the Holy Spirit make it easy if we follow them. It becomes difficult when we try to do it ourselves. When the flesh takes over and doesn't yield to the Spirit. We must yield to Jesus and the Spirit and trust in them to work through our lives, "*Come to Me, all you who labor and are heavy laden, and I will give you rest. Take My yoke upon you and learn from Me, for I am gentle and lowly in heart, and you will find rest for your souls. For My yoke is easy and My burden is light.*" (Matthew 11:28–30 NKJV)

Christianity is hard because we must give control of our lives to the

Holy Spirit. The Holy Spirit is our helper, guide, teacher and He lives inside us. Jesus provided the Holy Spirit to be with us in His absence. Yet, we must yield to the Holy Spirit. He will not force Himself on us. We must let Him have control of us. The Holy Spirit is a key part to growing our faith. The Holy Spirit lives inside us. He teaches, instructs, and intercedes on behalf of the believers. The Father provided the Spirit to us, "*the Spirit of truth, whom the world cannot receive, because it neither sees Him nor knows Him; but you know Him, for He dwells with you and will be in you.*" (John 14:17 NKJV)

God has made us all priests by birthright, "*But you are a chosen generation, a royal priesthood, a holy nation, His own special people, that you may proclaim the praises of Him who called you out of darkness into His marvelous light.*" (1 Peter 2:9 NKJV) When we are born again, we became a priest. Priests have direct access to God. We can petition Him directly through our prayers. Both Jesus, as the High Priest, and the Holy Spirit will intercede for us. (Heb 7:25, Rom 8:26 NKJV) When we pray, we ought to pray that Jesus and the Holy Spirit intercede for us.

Tithing is a form of worship. The relationship needs to get to a point where tithing is a joy. We can't wait to be able to have the opportunity to tithe again: to be able to give the money back to the Lord. Giving gifts makes us feel special inside. The Lord enjoys giving the money to us. He especially enjoys when we give back so His Gospel can reach others. It brings glory to His name and shows our proper respect for Him. That is where the relationship needs to reach.

Christianity is hard because people could ruin tithing for us because it feels like we are giving the money to people. But if we are tithing and believe that it is a bible-believing church, then we are doing the right thing. It is in the Lord's hands then and God help the people who aren't good stewards of that money. Our only part is to tithe. We are giving the money back to God, not the people in the church. When we write out the checks, we ought to imagine that we are writing God in the to: line when in reality we are writing the name of the church. We must remember that and pray that they will use it properly and for the glory of God. Our role is to tithe. Their role is to be good stewards of the resources. Don't let people stop us from tithing or serving because then they are getting between us and God. It is affecting our relationship with God. We shouldn't let any person stop us from worshipping God with our tithes, gifts, or service. This is difficult and takes a lot of love. This also can be applied to service.

> Personal application – Christianity is hard because I would rather say that I am a follower of Jesus Christ than be called religious. I say I am a man of strong faith. I believe Jesus is the Son of God. He is my Savior. He is my King. I want to focus the conversation on Jesus and the relationship I have with Him. Not about the church or the rules of religion. My faith is all about a relationship. Having said that, I do believe that community is important part of the faith journey. Church when functioning correctly works well and can be a place of spiritual renewal and growth. Church needs to focus on the head of the church, which is Jesus Christ. More on this in the chapter on Loving Others.

Christianity is hard because it appears that God has a different relationship with everyone. Other believers interact with God differently. Yes we all pray, read our bible, worship, and otherwise demonstrate our love for God. Each of us worship and interact with the Trinity in different ways. Based on our experiences and faith level, some talk only to God the Father, while others talk mainly to Jesus and others to the Holy Spirit.

God the Father, God the Son, and God the Holy Spirit desire to be in a deep and fulfilling relationship with us. Pray that we would accept their offer today and every day after today.

Devotional – Love of the Father

As a father, my kids ask what I want for Father's Day. My standard answer has been: "The love and adoration of my children." That is what is most important to me. Material things are a nice gesture, but what I really want is to spend time with them and for them to want to spend time with me. I cherish that time.

Then I realized that God the Father wants to spend time with me and for me to want to spend time with Him, "*And I heard a loud voice from heaven saying, 'Behold, the tabernacle of God is with men, and He will dwell with them, and they shall be His people. God Himself will be with them and be their God.'*" (Rev 21:3 NKJV)

Have you ever cried out to Abba Father? This title signifies a close, intimate relationship of a father to his child, as well as the childlike trust that a young child puts in his "daddy." God wants to be my God. He wants to love me as His kid, "*But as it is written: Eye has not seen, nor ear heard, nor have entered into the heart of man the things which God has prepared for those who love Him.*" (1Cor2:9 NKJV)

Call out to Abba Father. He wants your love and adoration this Father's Day and every day. Spend some time with Him. Love Him. Adore Him. It will be time well spent!

My prayer for this day, "*Now may the Lord direct your hearts into the love of God and into the patience of Christ.*" (2Thes 3:5 NKJV)

CHAPTER 6

JESUS IS ENOUGH

"Who is this King of glory? The LORD strong and mighty, The LORD mighty in battle. Lift up your heads, O your gates! Lift up, you everlasting doors! And the King of glory shall come in. Who is this King of glory? The LORD of hosts, He is the King of glory Selah."

PSALM 24:8–10 NKJV

Christianity is hard because we have trouble accepting that Jesus is everything. Jesus is our King, Lord, and Savior. Jesus is everything. He created us, *"All things were created through Him and for Him. And He is before all things, and in Him all things consist."* (Colossians 1:16b–17 NKJV) He is the perfect High Priest, perfect sacrifice, perfect covenant, perfect tabernacle. He lived a sinless life. He loved perfectly. He offers this to us today. We only need to accept it; do you believe it?

Jesus is more than words can describe. This book cannot adequately cover what Jesus means to us. Words just don't do it justice. When we say that Jesus is enough and is everything, then how do we begin to describe or write about it? For example, there are many attributes of Jesus Christ that appear to conflict with each other. He is God and Man at the same time. He is described as a Lion and a Lamb. He is the Alpha and Omega.

He is a King but came to serve. He is the Savior and the Judge. He is Life and yet He died for our sins. He is not bound by time or space. Jesus made all things, *"All things were made through Him, and without Him nothing was made that was made."* (John 1:3 NKJV) And, *"For of Him and through Him and to Him are all things, to whom be glory forever."* (Romans 11:36 NKJV)

> Personal application – Frankly, this is a hard chapter to write for me. Jesus is too wonderful, too perfect for one to fully grasp or know how to relate to His supremacy in all things. I fall woefully short and am unworthy. Only through Jesus can I write this book. I can do nothing without Jesus, *"for without Me you can do nothing."* (John 15:5 NKJV) Having said all that, by the grace of God I will try to capture what Jesus means to me and why it is hard to be His disciple.

Christianity is hard because it requires that we willingly commit our life to Christ. It is a choice. Discipleship costs us everything. Halving our effort with God results in frustration and confusion. We can't have it both ways. We are inherently selfish. We want it our way. We can either accept Christ and all His ways completely or not. It's not about only accepting the tenets that we want and dismiss the hard ones.

Jesus wants to be our King. There was a time when the Israelites wanted to be like all the other nations. Samuel was Israel's leader as a Judge. Up until this point in the life of Israel as nation, they only had judges and not a king. Israel demanded to have a king appointed over them and to rule them. If they had only known that they already had a King, a heavenly King. But the Israelites wanted an earthly king like all the other nations, *"Now make us a king to judge us like all the nations."* (1 Samuel 8:5b NKJV) This displeased Samuel and he cried out to the Lord, *"And the LORD said to Samuel, 'Heed the voice of the people in all that they say to you; for they have not rejected you, but they have rejected Me, that I should not reign over them.'"* (1 Samuel 8:7 NKJV) The Lord took this as a rejection of His leadership. God loves us enough to give us the desires of our heart, even if it will hurt us. Samuel then explains what having an earthly king will mean. It isn't good. Be careful what we ask for.

Jesus wants to be our King just like He wanted to be Israel's King. Israel's history of man in relation to our Lord is telling of how much love God has for us. It also tells how much patience God has for His people. He won't force Himself on us. He provides His leadership freely to us, but we must accept it. We must willingly fall under His rule and Lordship to be part of His Kingdom. The Lord will wait for His people to accept Him. For them to realize their need of salvation and have a clear understanding of their need for Him. If we have ever felt rejection from someone dear to us, then we can begin to understand the level of hurt. Pray that we accept Jesus as our King today.

Christianity is hard because we can't earn our way to salvation. Pride is the downfall of many. We can't do anything to restore the relationship except to believe in Jesus and accept the gift. We need to get out of the way and let Jesus save us.

Jesus is our Savior. "*For there is born to you this day in the city of David a Savior, who is Christ the Lord.*" (Luke 2:11 NKJV) We need a Savior to save us from ourselves and our sins. Ever since the fall in the garden, we have needed a way to restore the relationship. Jesus provided us that way. He has provided a way for us to be saved from our sins, "*And you shall call His name Jesus, for He will save His people from their sins.*" (Matthew 1:21b NKJV) By accepting Jesus, the relationship is restored, and we become citizens of heaven, "*For our citizenship is in heaven, from which we also eagerly wait for the Savior, the Lord Jesus Christ.*" (Philippians 3:20 NKJV) Thank You God for sending Your Son Jesus to save us. We needed it.

Jesus came to save us from our sins and return us to a relationship to the Father. Jesus states this in the book of Mark, "*The time is fulfilled, and the kingdom of God is at hand. Repent, and believe in the gospel.*" (Mark 1:15 NKJV) A key to the faith is to believe. It restores the broken relationship with God the Father through His Son Jesus Christ.

Jesus is the Word of God, "*And the Word became flesh and dwelt* among us, and we beheld His glory, the glory as of the only begotten of the Father, full of grace and truth." (John 1:14 NKJV) Jesus was at creation, "In the beginning was the Word, and the Word was with God, and the Word was God. He was in the beginning with God. All things were made through Him, and without Him nothing was made that was made." (John 1:1–3 NKJV) This is another concept that takes faith to understand and grasp. It takes faith to understand that the Word of God is the Incarnate Christ. And just as Jesus was there in the beginning, He will be there at Judgment day, "He was clothed with a robe dipped in blood, and His name is called The Word of God." (Revelation 19:13 NKJV)

Christianity is hard because we are no longer ours. Jesus is our Lord. This means that we are owned by Jesus Christ. He has redeemed us from our sins and now we owe Him our life. We are bondservants to Him. He can do with us as He pleases. But it isn't like we are miserable in this relationship. It is quite the opposite. Jesus is a loving master. We are to love Him back. He has freed us from being slaves to sin. In return, we ought to honor and glorify Him as Lord. We are to obey His word. We can choose to freely give our life back to Him and serve Him with all our heart, soul, and mind.

Christianity is hard because we are in the process of changing. God gives us a new heart to know that Jesus is Lord, "Then I will give them a heart to know Me, that I am the LORD; and they shall be My people, and I will be their God, for they shall return to Me with their whole heart." (Jeremiah 24:7 NKJV) To not understand that Jesus can do with us as He pleases is to be naïve in spiritual matters. He is Lord and we will eventually confess that He is Lord, "and that every tongue should confess that Jesus Christ is Lord, to the glory of God the Father." (Philippians 2:11 NKJV) Having said that, it would be best to choose to accept the gift of salvation offered by Jesus. He will give us a new heart and change us from within, if we let Him. It is a choice, nonetheless.

Lordship also means that we are free and safe to live in His Kingdom, "And the Lord will deliver me from every evil work and preserve me for His heavenly kingdom." (2 Timothy 4:18a NKJV) If we have accepted Jesus as our King and submitted to Him as Lord, then the Kingdom of God is within us, "*The kingdom of God does not come with observation; nor will they say, 'See here!' or 'See there!' For indeed, the kingdom of God is within you.*" (Luke 17:21 NKJV) We can experience the Kingdom of God now. This is what Jesus means when He says, "*And the peace of God, which surpasses all understanding, will guard your hearts and minds through Christ Jesus.*" (Philippians 4:7 NKJV) Our priority should be to seek His Kingdom, "*Seek first the kingdom of God and His righteousness, and all these things shall be added to you.*" (Matthew 6:33 NKJV)

Jesus is our redeemer. God sent Jesus to redeem us and adopt us as sons, "*to redeem those who were under the law, that we might receive the adoption as sons.*" (Galatians 4:5 NKJV) Jesus paid the price for our sins. Jesus, as our High Priest, entered the Holy of Holies, to present the perfect sacrifice, Himself, "*Not with the blood of goats and calves, but with His own blood He entered the Most Holy Place once for all, having obtained eternal redemption.*" (Hebrews 9:12 NKJV) His perfect sacrifice satisfied the debt we owe for all our sins and restored us as sons. "*But this Man (Jesus), after He had offered one sacrifice for sins forever, sat down at the right hand of God.*" (Hebrews 10:12 NKJV) Therefore, one of the names for Jesus is Lamb of God.

Jesus is the Judge. One day Jesus will judge us, "*in the day when God will judge the secrets of men by Jesus Christ, according to my gospel.*" (Romans 2:16 NKJV) If we have accepted Jesus as our Lord and Savior, then we will be spared the judgment, "*Then we who are alive and remain shall be caught up together with them in the clouds to meet the Lord in the air. And thus we shall always be with the Lord.*" (1 Thessalonians 4:17 NKJV) And for those who haven't accepted Jesus, it is the lake of fire for you, "*And anyone not found written in the Book of Life was cast into the lake of fire.*" (Revelation 20:15 NKJV) Jesus gives us a choice. And with any choice, there is a consequence. In this case, it is either the lake of fire or in heaven with Jesus. It isn't God's desire for anyone to spend eternity in hell. He gives us the choice. Even though it isn't His desire, He will let anyone live with their choice.

Christianity is hard because relating to Jesus is different based on our heart. Are we relating to the graceful Jesus who bestows forgiveness and saves us from our sins? Are we relating to the Jesus who is Lord of lords and Kings of kings? Are we relating to the Judge? Are we relating to the Savior? Jesus dealt with everyone according to their faith. If they were humble and submitted to His Lordship through faith, He would work miracles in their lives. If they were arrogant and proud, He would feel compassion on them, but let them live in their ignorance. He loved them enough to give them the choice.

Let's compare three different stories of how Jesus related to different people. Here is an example of a humble person of great faith. The centurion's story is captured in Matt 8:5-10 NKJV. The centurion pleads with Jesus to heal his servant. First, admire the compassion of the centurion for his servant. Once Jesus agrees to come to the centurion's house to heal the servant, "The centurion answered and said, '*Lord, I am not worthy that You should come under my roof. But only speak a word, and my servant will be healed.*'" (Matthew 8:8 NKJV) When Jesus heard it, He marveled, and said to those who followed, "*Assuredly, I say to you, I have not found such great faith, not even in Israel!*" (Matthew 8:10 NKJV) Jesus heals the servant by just telling the centurion that his servant is healed.

Compare the centurion's great faith to the unbelief of the people from Jesus' "own country." Jesus returns to where He grew up and the people do not believe in Him. Here again Jesus marvels at the actions of humans. This time it is because of unbelief and not a great faith, "*And He marveled because of their unbelief.*" (Mark 6:6 NKJV) This resulted in Jesus not doing many works there because of their unbelief, "*Now He could do no mighty work there.*" (Mark 6:5a NKJV) Jesus relates to everyone based on their faith.

Next comparison. There is a lady asking Jesus to have mercy on her daughter who is demon-possessed. Jesus responds with, "*It is not good to take the children's bread and throw it to the little dogs.*" (Matthew 15:26 NKJV) The lady's humble response, "*Yes, Lord, yet even the little dogs eat the crumbs which fall from their masters' table.*" (Matthew 15:27 NKJV)

"*Then Jesus answered and said to her, 'O woman, great is your faith! Let it be to you as you desire.' And her daughter was healed from that very hour.*" (Matthew 15:28 NKJV)

Compare this with the Pharisees and Sadducees. They kept trying to test Jesus to see if He would provide them a sign from heaven, "*testing Him asked that He would show them a sign from heaven.*" (Matthew 16:1b NKJV) They were showing no faith and were being arrogant in their testing. Jesus responds to them, "'*A wicked and adulterous generation seeks after a sign, and no sign shall be given to it except the sign of the prophet Jonah.' And He left them and departed.*" (Matthew 16:4 NKJV) Jesus let them live in their ignorance.

The third comparison. First is the call of Levi (Matthew). Levi was a rich tax collector. Jesus calls to Levi and says, "*Follow Me*" (Luke 5:27b NKJV) And then the Bible says, "*So he left all, rose up, and followed Him.*" (Luke 5:28 NKJV) Levi left all. He submitted to the Lordship of Jesus.

Compare this with the rich ruler who desires to find eternal life, "*Good Teacher, what shall I do to inherit eternal life?*" (Luke 18:18 NKJV) Jesus responds to keep the commandments. The ruler responds that he has kept them since his youth. Jesus then says, "*You still lack one thing. Sell all that you have and distribute to the poor, and you will have treasure in heaven; and come, follow Me.*" (Luke 18:22 NKJV) This was a special invite. Jesus didn't invite all to follow Him but told them to go and tell folks of His love. The ruler's response is the opposite of Levi's response, "*But when he heard this, he became very sorrowful, for he was very rich.*" (Luke 18:23 NKJV) He was not willing to submit to the Lordship of Jesus Christ. Jesus lets the ruler live with his choice.

Christianity is hard because Jesus deals with each us differently so there isn't one key answer to following Christ. He has a different plan for each of us. Much of the process is the same, but each of us handle it in our own unique way.

Christianity is hard because we try many different paths rather than going through Jesus. Living through Christ isn't natural by our worldly standards. It goes against the things we have been taught. Self-dependence.

Do not rely on anyone else. If we want something, we need to do it ourselves. Jesus says there is no other way, "*Jesus said to him, 'I am the way, the truth, and the life. No one comes to the Father except through Me.'*" (John 14:6 NKJV)

Through Jesus, God has provided us everything we need. Through Jesus Christ our Lord we have faith (Acts 15:11 NKJV), redemption (Rom 3:24 NKJV), love (Titus 3:4–6 NKJV), peace (Rom 5:1, Phil 4:7 NKJV), reconciliation (Rom 5:11 NKJV), righteousness (Rom 5:17 NKJV), new life (1Cor 8:6 NKJV), victory (1Cor 15:57 NKJV), triumph (2Cor 2:14 NKJV), trust (2Cor 3:4 NKJV), salvation (1Th 5:9 NKJV), hope (1Pet 1:3 NKJV), grace (Jn 1:17 NKJV), truth (Jn 1:17 NKJV), and all things (1Cor 8:6, Eph 3:9 NKJV). Through Christ we are rich (2Cor 8:9 NKJV), wise (2Tim 3:15 NKJV), complete (Heb 13:21 NKJV), a child of God (Gal 3:26 NKJV), and an Heir (Gal 4:7 NKJV). Please take the time to research and read each one of these passages. Let the word of God sink deep into our heart that Jesus is enough.

Jesus loves us and wants a relationship with us. He wants to help us walk through life. He wants us to enjoy life to the fullest. What is keeping you from experiencing Jesus today?

Devotional – The Joy of the Lord

"*These things I have spoken unto you that My joy might remain in you and that your joy might be full.*" (John 15:11 NKJV) These things Jesus speaks of are abiding in His love and loving others as we rely on His strength and wisdom, "*for without Jesus you can do nothing.*" (John 15:5 NKJV)

Many Christians don't feel or experience the joy of the Lord. They live under a cloud of disappointment because they have been robbed of their joy. Paul learned that the secret to joy is found in the way a Christian thinks, "*for I have learned in whatever state I am, to be content.*" (Philippians 4:11b NKJV) I can still hear my mom saying, "You can get glad just as easy as you got mad." Let's look at the four thieves that rob Christians of their joy.

Circumstances – We can't control the circumstances that come in our life, but we don't have to let them control us. We can control our reaction to them. Here are just two examples in the Bible dealing with circumstances. After being beaten and jailed for preaching Jesus, the apostles *"rejoiced that they were counted worthy to suffer shame for His name."* (Acts 5:41 NKJV) Paul's reaction to being placed in jail is looking at the world bigger than his immediate surroundings, *"that the things which happened to me have actually turned out for the furtherance of the gospel."* (Phil 1:12 NKJV) Your reaction to circumstances is a demonstration of your faith. It is at times like this that you must put your life in the hands of the Lord. You get the grace (joy) and He gets the glory.

People – Have you ever met someone who is an EGR (Extra Grace Required)? When you realize that you are an EGR, then it helps you look at people differently. Jesus loves them too. When you think you are all that, how much more grace do you require? *"Let nothing be done through selfish ambition or conceit, but in lowliness of mind let each esteem others better than himself."* (Philippians 2:3 NKJV) Everyone is valuable to the Lord and so it shall be with us also. We are all EGRs and the more grace and love we can show each other will go a long way to helping everyone's joy to increase, including your own, *"Let each of you look out not only for his own interests, but also for the interests of others."* (Philippians 2:4 NKJV)

Worry – Have you ever experienced the peace of God? Nothing will get you down when you are walking with the Lord and close to Him. It is a wonderful thing. Worry is the opposite of faith. Jesus commands us to not worry, *"Therefore I say to you, do not worry about your life, what you will eat or what you will drink; nor about your body, what you will put on. Is not life more than food and the body more than clothing?"* (Matthew 6:25 NKJV) Don't let worry steal your joy. Phil 4:6–7 NKJV states, *"Be anxious for nothing, but in everything by prayer and supplication, with thanksgiving, let your requests be made known to God; and the peace of God, which surpasses all understanding, will guard your hearts and minds through Christ Jesus."* God is able. Do you believe?

Things – Are you a material girl? Or boy? Do you define yourself by your things? You can never get enough. Solomon was a king who had everything. He writes in (Eccl 2:10 NKJV), *"Whatever my eyes desired I did not keep from them. I did not withhold my heart from any pleasure."* He concluded in verse 11, *"Indeed all was vanity and grasping for the wind. There was no profit under the sun."* Jesus warns us about having too much stuff in Luke 12:15 NKJV, *"Take heed and beware of covetousness, for one's life does not consist in the abundance of the things he possesses."* We have already received the best present anyone could receive. The gift that the Lord Jesus has given to us. And we can enjoy it every day! Not just on Christmas. Jesus is enough.

When you abide in His love and love others, you will experience the joy of the Lord. I pray that the world would overflow with His love and joy. *"These things I have spoken unto you that My joy might remain in you and that your joy might be full."* (John 15:11 NKJV)

CHAPTER 7

FELLOWSHIP OF HIS SUFFERINGS

"That I may know Him and the power of His resurrection, and the fellowship of His sufferings, being conformed to His death."

(PHILIPPIANS 3:10 NKJV)

C hristianity is hard because we will share in the sufferings of Christ, *"that I may know Him and the power of His resurrection, and the fellowship of His sufferings, being conformed to His death."* (Philippians 3:10 NKJV) Why? Why do we have to suffer? It is part of being the disciple of Jesus Christ, *"For to you it has been granted on behalf of Christ, not only to believe in Him, but also to suffer for His sake."* (Philippians 1:29 NKJV)

God uses suffering to perfect us. God will use the suffering to mold us into His likeness, *"For it was fitting for Him, for whom are all things and by whom are all things, in bringing many sons to glory, to make the captain of their salvation perfect through sufferings."* (Hebrews 2:10 NKJV)

Some Christians relish in their sufferings. They wear it around like a badge of honor. Others shy away from any type of suffering, even though suffering will come. The Bible tells us to rejoice when we are being tried, *"Beloved, do not think it strange concerning the fiery trial which is to try you, as though some strange thing happened to you; but rejoice to the extent that you partake of Christ's sufferings, that when His glory is revealed, you may also be glad with exceeding joy."* (1 Peter 4:12–13 NKJV)

Christianity is hard when we try to do it ourselves. We need to lean on Jesus, "*Come to Me, all you who labor and are heavy laden, and I will give you rest. Take My yoke upon you and learn from Me, for I am gentle and lowly in heart, and you will find rest for your souls. For My yoke is easy and My burden is light.*" (Matthew 11:28–30 NKJV)

Christianity is hard because there are expectations that the Christian life is one of pure joy. Some Christians have expectations that the Christian life is going to be an easy blissful life where everything works out, "*And we know that all things work together for good to those who love God, to those who are the called according to His purpose.*" (Romans 8:28 NKJV)

While this can be the case from time to time, there are a couple of caveats. And when folks realize that it isn't all bliss, they fall away from the faith. Looking at Romans 8:28 NKJV, most people stop at "*all things work together for good.*" But the rest of the verse says, "*for those that love God,*" which means that they will obey Him "*for this is the love of God, that we keep His commandments. And His commandments are not burdensome.*" (1 John 5:3 NKJV) We, as the people of God, are not very good at obeying; just saying.

Romans 8:28 also says according to God's purpose. God's purpose for our life may not be to our liking. God's purpose for Job was to be used to make a point with Satan and a lesson for us in which Job lost everything but his life. God's purpose in the rich man's life was for him to sell everything and follow Christ. (Matt 19:21 NKJV) God's purpose for Joseph was to be sold into slavery so he could become the leader in Egypt. The Bible presents many examples of God's purpose in people's life. In each of the examples, there are specific circumstances related to each person that detail God's purpose for their life. Each person has a specific purpose for their life. We all have a general purpose. And that is to glorify God.

Christianity is hard because the gate is narrow and the way difficult. Narrow gate – What? Why? Why is the gate narrow? "*Enter by the narrow gate; for wide is the gate and broad is the way that leads to destruction, and there are many who go in by it. Because narrow is the gate and difficult is the way which leads to life, and there are few who find it.*" (Matthew

7:13–14 NKJV) Doesn't God want all to be saved? *"God desires all men to be saved and to come to the knowledge of the truth."* (1 Timothy 2:4 NKJV) Then why is the gate narrow? If God wants all to be saved, why is it so hard? Didn't God create us? He could have created us and made the way easier, right? So then, why the narrow gate?

The gate isn't narrow because God wants to limit how many people walk through the gate. The gate is narrow because only so many will make the choice to follow the Shepherd in total dependence. There will not be many who find the gate, *"Strive to enter through the narrow gate, for many, I say to you, will seek to enter and will not be able."* (Luke 13:24 NKJV) God wants all of us. He doesn't want just half of us or when we think it is convenient. That is why the gate is narrow because only a few will give all to Him, *"So likewise, whoever of you does not forsake all that he has cannot be My disciple."* (Luke 14:33 NKJV)

Christianity is hard because suffering comes with faith. This is unfortunate but true. This passage from Hebrews shows the level of suffering that the heroes of faith endured as part of their faith journey, *"And what more shall I say? For the time would fail me to tell of Gideon and Barak and Samson and Jephthah, also of David and Samuel and the prophets: who through faith subdued kingdoms, worked righteousness, obtained promises, stopped the mouths of lions, quenched the violence of fire, escaped the edge of the sword, out of weakness were made strong, became valiant in battle, turned to fight the armies of the aliens. Women received their dead raised to life again. And others were tortured, not accepting deliverance, that they might obtain a better resurrection. Still others had trial of mockings and scourgings, yes, and of chains and imprisonment. They were stoned, they were sawn in two, were tempted, were slain with the sword. They wandered about in sheepskins and goatskins, being destitute, afflicted, tormented of whom the world was not worthy. They wandered in deserts and mountains, in dens and caves of the earth."* (Hebrews 11:32–38 NKJV)

The world was not worthy for these heroes of faith. They are listed here to encourage us in our time of suffering.

Jesus provides the example as documented in Hebrews for us to strive against our sins. Have we resisted against sin to the level of bloodshed? *"For consider Him who endured such hostility from sinners against Himself, lest you become weary and discouraged in your souls. You have not yet resisted to bloodshed, striving against sin."* (Hebrews 12:3–4 NKJV) This verse is convicting about our efforts to follow Jesus. The ironic part about this statement is that we can't beat our sin. We can only have victories over our sin through Jesus. The striving for us then becomes our ability to battle our sins through the word and strength of Jesus. We must use the armor of God to fight these battles (Eph 6:11–17 NKJV)

Jesus provides two parables about the difficulty of being a Christian and the cost of discipleship. First is about a builder of house. He first calculates if he has enough to finish the job before he even starts. The second talks about a king and whether he will win a battle. (Luke 14:28–32 NKJV) The parables point out that we should calculate the cost of following Jesus and being a Christian. It is hard, costly, and the gate is narrow.

Christianity is hard because God wants all of us. God doesn't like halfhearted people. Here is what the Lord says to the church at Laodicea, *"I know your works, that you are neither cold nor hot. I could wish you were cold or hot. So then, because you are lukewarm, and neither cold nor hot, I will vomit you out of My mouth."* (Revelation 3:15–16 NKJV)

Personal application – At one of the churches I attended, there was an associate pastor leading the hosting of a homeless shelter for a week. As he gathered volunteers, he wanted to test their commitment. As part of the training to volunteer for the shelter, he purposely made it painful to see who would stick it out. This made no sense to me at the time. I cautioned him that if someone was available and willing to provide an hour, then he should be thankful and welcome the person. He would rather work with a few completely dedicated than many halfhearted people. I thought it was important to work with people at their level of spiritual maturity and encourage them to grow into being completely dedicated.

These two approaches highlight the complexity within the Christian community on the approaches to following Christ. How do we know which one was right? At the time of the dialogue, I thought I was so right (as usual if you ask people who know me) But now after some additional insight, he may have been correct, in a way. I think both approaches are needed. It is the way Christ handles people who want to be His disciples. Christ will accept you and save you once you accept His gift of grace. He will also work with you at your level of faith. But to follow Christ and be used by Him is another matter completely. We need to be completely His and submit to His leadership. There will be suffering and some pain along the way. He loves you and will accept you as a child of God, but to be used by Him requires commitment.

Christianity is hard because the Holy Spirit is going to change us. Once we are saved by accepting Christ as our Lord and Savior, then the Holy Spirit will start to change us from the inside if we let Him, *"But we … are being transformed into the same image from glory to glory, just as by the Spirit of the Lord."* (2 Corinthians 3:18 NKJV) The key here is to let Him change us. We must willingly let the Spirit guide our life. It is no longer our life but God's. It takes faith to change. It seems that it has taken a lifetime. And He still isn't finished. This could be yet another point of falling away. Faith takes work. It needs to be nourished daily if not hourly. The Holy Spirit has His work cut out for a sort like us. It is a constant battle of wills. Even though we know that it is the right answer, we press on, *"Not that I have already attained, or am already perfected; but I press on, that I may lay hold of that for which Christ Jesus has also laid hold of me."* (Philippians 3:12 NKJV) Sometimes the Holy Spirit changes us through sufferings.

Christianity is hard because we have three enemies that afflict us in our suffering. They are the world, Satan, and our flesh. All three can pull us away from God. And we will suffer for it.

The Bible warns us of the world, "*Do not love the world or the things in the world. If anyone loves the world, the love of the Father is not in him. For all that is in the world—the lust of the flesh, the lust of the eyes, and the pride of life—is not of the Father but is of the world.*" (1 John 2:15–16 NKJV)

Satan prowls around seeing who he can destroy, "*Be sober, be vigilant; because your adversary the devil walks about like a roaring lion, seeking whom he may devour.*" (1 Peter 5:8 NKJV)

The flesh represents our sin nature, "*For I know that in me (that is, in my flesh) nothing good dwells; for to will is present with me, but how to perform what is good I do not find.*" (Romans 7:18 NKJV)

The key is to walk in the Spirit, "*I say then: Walk in the Spirit, and you shall not fulfill the lust of the flesh. For the flesh lusts against the Spirit, and the Spirit against the flesh; and these are contrary to one another, so that you do not do the things that you wish.*" (Galatians 5:16–17 NKJV) Submit to God and Satan will flee from us, "*Therefore submit to God. Resist the devil and he will flee from you.*" (James 4:7 NKJV)

Christianity is hard because Jesus is the only way, "*Jesus said to him, 'I am the way, the truth, and the life. No one comes to the Father except through Me.'*" (John 14:6 NKJV) We have tried many other ways. While we don't have the resources that Solomon had to test everything under the sun, we have had plenty of opportunities to test many roads, paths, and gates. And just like in Ecclesiastes (Eccl 12:13–14), the same conclusion materializes: God is the only way. We have been down the other paths and we know where they lead.

So then, what are our choices?

1. To just live and then puff, we are gone. There is no hope in that approach. Life has no meaning. This is a sad way to live. There is no purpose to life.
2. To purposely live for Satan. This approach leads to destruction and eternity in the lake of fire, "*The devil, who deceived them, was cast into the lake of fire and brimstone where the beast and the*

false prophet are. And they will be tormented day and night forever and ever." (Revelation 20:10 NKJV)

3. To unwittingly choose Satan. This approach has the same result as purposely living for Satan, even though it wasn't a specific choice. To not choose is making a choice, *"And anyone not found written in the Book of Life was cast into the lake of fire."* (Revelation 20:15 NKJV)

4. To choose God. This approach leads to eternal life, *"that whoever believes in Him should not perish but have eternal life."* (John 3:15 NKJV)

So, then, we get mad at God and want to throw this whole thing called faith out the door. And we say to ourselves, we will just go back to doing nothing and maybe we will be left alone. We get frustrated that it is too hard and want to quit. Through trials, sufferings and victories we realize the only real choice is to choose God. He loves us. He wants to be our God and for us to be His children.

"For I consider that the sufferings of this present time are not worthy to be compared with the glory which shall be revealed in us." (Romans 8:18 NKJV)

CHAPTER 8

FEAR OF THE LORD

"The fear of the LORD is the beginning of wisdom, And the knowl-edge of the Holy One is understanding."

C hristianity is hard because we are to fear the Lord. The phrase *"the fear of the Lord"* is used throughout the Bible. There are two common understandings of fear. The first is the fear that God will exercise judgment on us. This is the wrath of God and the fear of it. The second is the fear that God is an awesome God and therefore we should be in awe of God's glory and majesty. In both cases, one should respect that God is God the Almighty, Maker of the universe (and us).

So, which is it: In awe of God or in a state of being afraid of God? There are cases where each is applicable. We are told to fear God, *"saying with a loud voice, 'Fear God and give glory to Him, for the hour of His judgment has come.'"* (Revelation 14:7a NKJV) And we are told to not fear God, *"Do not fear, little flock, for it is your Father's good pleasure to give you the kingdom."* (Luke 12:32 NKJV) As with all the other things in this relationship, it is all about the heart and intent. If we are walking with the Lord and accepted Him as Savior, then we have nothing to fear and we are in awe. If we are unrepentant, disrespectful, and disobedient, then we have a lot to fear and should be scared. It depends on the state of our relationship with God.

The fear (afraid) of the Lord is the understanding that it is the beginning of wisdom, that we don't deserve grace, that a holy God deserves justice. That He controls everything in our life. That He could destroy us as in the days of the flood. That His discipline is true, quick, and just.

The fear (awe) of the Lord is also the understanding that He freely gives us His grace, that He died to redeem us and take our punishment. That He wants us to follow Him in obedience. That He desires to fellowship with us. That we have victory through Him. That His love is patient, complete, and never fails.

Fear is tightly related to wisdom and understanding in the Bible, "*The fear of the LORD is the beginning of wisdom; A good understanding have all those who do His commandments. His praise endures forever.*" (Psalm 111:10 NKJV)

Every person can experience both types of fear. This verse from Hebrews shows that we should have both the reverential awe and Godly fear, "*Therefore, since we are receiving a kingdom which cannot be shaken, let us have grace, by which we may serve God acceptably with reverence and godly fear. For our God is a consuming fire.*" (Hebrews 12:28–29 NKJV) Even though this is from a section of the Bible that talks about the judgment of God, it talks about the grace that saves us and empowers us to serve a living God with both awe and Godly fear. God is going to cleanse all our impurities with fire (1 Cor 3:12–15 NKJV) And the things which can't be shaken will remain. And those unshakeable things are our relationship with Jesus, the rock of our salvation.

We are one with Christ when we are no longer afraid of what the world has for us. When we properly fear (awe) God, then we will have nothing left to fear from the world. When we consider all that God has done for us, then the only response is to be in fear (awe) of Him. God sent His only Son to take our penalty for sin. And that penalty was death. That is how much God loves us, "*Greater love has no one than this, than to lay down one's life for his friends.*" (John 15:13 NKJV) Once we comprehend the extent of God's love for us, then the true love of God can cast out fear, *"There is no fear in love; but perfect love casts out fear, because fear involves torment. But he who fears has not been made perfect in love."* (1 John 4:18 NKJV) Love removes the fear.

It is out of fear that many people come to God; fear of missing heaven, fear of hell, fear of Satan, fear of eternity, fear of the judgment. Many pastors use this technique during their sermons. They scare the people into being saved. If that fear doesn't turn into love, then the salvation has a limited chance of surviving. For many, that confession does turn into love, but for the rest, the motivation for being saved is wrong. Therefore, one would have to question whether it was a real confession from the heart, *"For with the heart one believes unto righteousness, and with the mouth confession is made unto salvation."* (Romans 10:10 NKJV) A person should come to Christ out of love and awe over His finished work of the cross. He saved us from our sins. We should be thankful of that fact and not be scared that He will judge us. If we deny Christ, then we should be fearful (afraid) of the judgment that will come.

The beginning of our understanding of the Lord, and therefore wisdom, begins with the fact that we will one day kneel before a Holy God. God is a righteous God and will exercise judgment on everyone. This should make us fearful (afraid) of that day. As we work out our salvation, that day becomes less fearful because of our positional standing before God through His Son, Jesus Christ. Once we accept Jesus as our savior (not only from this Day of Judgment), then we begin to understand God's plan. It is for us to love Him as the loving God. As we begin to love Jesus more and more each day, then that fear becomes awe. Once a soul understands that God can totally control their life at any point and His judgment is complete, then that is the beginning of wisdom. That is where knowledge starts. This needs to be the basis to all our thinking.

God controls everything in our life if we are His, *"Indeed those who are under the control of the flesh cannot please God. You, however, are not of the flesh but under the control of the Spirit, since God's Spirit lives in you. And if anyone does not have the Spirit of Christ, he does not belong* to him." (Romans 8:8–9 NKJV) God allows Satan to control us if we are part of this world, "*who were dead in trespasses and sins, in which you once walked according to the course of this world, according to the prince of the power of the air, the spirit who now works in the sons of disobedience.*" (Ephesians 2:1b–2 NKJV) To not understand that God is a righteous God is to create folly in our life. Acknowledging that God controls everything is important in our walk of faith. We can do nothing of ourselves. God can make us a success or a failure.

> Personal application – Christianity is hard because we are to live out of the love of God and not out of fear of Him. I have experienced the discipline of God enough times to fear it. Yes, that is right, I fear (scared) the discipline of God. Even though all my sins were forgiven at the cross, there remains a consequence of sin. He disciplines those He loves, "*For whom the LORD loves He chastens, And scourges every son whom He receives.*" (Hebrews 12:6 NKJV) He wants the best for us. It is meant to bring us in alignment with His love and will. And it works. It keeps me from sinning because I know that the Lord will correct me. The discipline of the Lord strengthens my faith. It is one of the strongest validations of my faith. I know He loves me because I am disciplined. I am disciplined because I am a child of God. I strive to love of God, "*Strive to enter through the narrow gate, for many, I say to you, will seek to enter and will not be able*" (Luke 13:24 NKJV).

This passage highlights when the word "fear" can be interpreted as "afraid." Jesus states, "*And I say to you, My friends, do not be afraid of those who kill the body, and after that have no more that they can do. But I will show you whom you should fear: Fear Him who, after He has killed, has power to cast into hell; yes, I say to you, fear Him!*" (Luke 12:4–5 NKJV)

Even the definition in *Strong's Concordance* uses both terms. So the argument goes that we should only look at the word as "awe" and not "afraid." Why should we be afraid of a loving all-knowing God? God is Love. Correct? Then what do we have to be afraid of? The answer is the judgment of God, "*And I saw the dead, small and great, standing before God, and books were opened. And another book was opened, which is the Book of Life. And the dead were judged according to their works, by the things which were written in the books. The sea gave up the dead who were in it, and Death and Hades delivered up the dead who were in them. And they were judged, each one according to his works. Then Death and Hades were cast into the lake of fire. This is the second death. And anyone not found written in the Book of Life was cast into the lake of fire.*" (Revelation 20:12–15 NKJV) If we are saved, then Jesus represents us at the judgment seat and our name is written in the Book of Life. If not, then we will be cast into the lake of fire.

When the Jewish people lost their fear of God and did what was right in their own eyes, their life took a turn for the worst. "*And it was so, at the beginning of their dwelling there, that they did not fear the LORD; therefore, the LORD sent lions among them, which killed some of them.*" (2 Kings 17:25 NKJV) This is repeated many times in the Old Testament where God is trying to get the attention of the Jewish people. This happens to us today. We leave God out of our lives and then wonder why these things are happening to us, "*The fear of the LORD is the beginning of knowledge, but fools despise wisdom and instruction.*" (Proverbs 1:7 NKJV) God is trying to get our attention. He wants to restore us to a relationship with Him. And then we shall know Him as Lord.

Here is an example of not fearing the Lord. Pharaoh did not fear the Lord and it cost him. He did not respect the fact that the Lord God could destroy his world. Pharaoh eventually understood (as we all will some-day) that the Lord God is in control, "*So Moses said to him, 'As soon as I have gone out of the city, I will spread out my hands to the LORD; the thunder will cease, and there will be no more hail, that you may know that the earth is the LORD'S. But as for you and your servants, I know that you will not yet fear the LORD God.'*" (Exodus 9:29–30 NKJV) And we know how this ended for Pharaoh. Egypt's army drowns in the Red Sea after chasing

Israel through the parting of it, "*Then the waters returned and covered the chariots, the horsemen, and all the army of Pharaoh that came into the sea after them. Not so much as one of them remained.*" (Exodus 14:28 NKJV) "*And then the Egyptians shall know that I am the Lord.*" (Exodus 14:18 NKJV)

Christianity is hard because the consequences of not fearing the Lord are eternal. We must understand the impact for a lack of fear of God. God explains to us that there are consequences for not choosing to fear the Lord, "*Then they will call on me, but I will not answer; They will seek me diligently, but they will not find me. Because they hated knowledge and did not choose the fear of the Lord. They would have none of my counsel and despised my every rebuke.*" (Proverbs 1:28–30 NKJV) It is interesting that it is a choice. We make choices every day, all day long. Opting not to choose is a choice. God gives us a free will to do as we please. How we choose then becomes very important. Understanding the consequences as stated in the Proverb becomes even more important. God will let us go to the devil, "*Deliver such a one to Satan for the destruction of the flesh, that his spirit may be saved in the day of the Lord Jesus.*" (1Cor 5:5 NKJV) Please note that not only will God not hear them nor answer them, but he also states that they don't even respond to his discipline. He must have rebuked this group of people and they would not listen. If we do not listen when the Lord is disciplining us and trying to get us to turn back to Him, then He may not listen when we finally realize our need of Him.

The fear of the Lord is many things, but to obtain the perspective that it relates to hating evil takes the understanding of the fear of the Lord to a new level of faith, "*The fear of the LORD is to hate evil, pride and arrogance and the evil way.*" (Proverbs 8:13 NKJV) To be so aligned with the Lord that anything that doesn't please the Lord also becomes displeasing to the individual is the level that we need to attain. This means that any sin that is nagging or entangling us needs to be brought into the light of discipline. That sin in our life is going to be dealt with at some point, and therefore we should fear the discipline of the Lord. It is coming, and He will desire that we deal with that sin. We need to remove it from our life.

The Lord will not help us if we are willfully sinning (Heb 10:26 NKJV). The sin in our life will continue to separate us from God. The Lord will try to bring us to repentance through circumstances in our life. Eventually if we don't repent, He will deliver us to Satan in hopes that our spirit will be saved. If we repent, then the Lord can bring us back into the fold and a relationship with Him. It is at that point that we should hate the evil that entangled us and created the separation from God.

We can be taught to fear the Lord. It doesn't come naturally to man to fear the Lord. He must be taught, "*Come, you children, listen to me; I will teach you the fear of the Lord.*" (Psalm 34:11 NKJV) As man begins to realize that there is an almighty God, he learns to fear God. We must respect and be in awe of God.

There are blessings and promises with fearing the Lord:

- "*The fear of the LORD prolongs days, but the years of the wicked will be shortened.*" (Proverbs 10:27 NKJV)
- "*In the fear of the LORD there is strong confidence, And His children will have a place of refuge. The fear of the LORD is a fountain of life, To turn one away from the snares of death.*" (Proverbs 14:26–27 NKJV)
- "*The fear of the LORD leads to life, and he who has it will abide in satisfaction; He will not be visited with evil.*" (Proverbs 19:23 NKJV)
- "*In mercy and truth atonement is provided for iniquity; and by the fear of the LORD one departs from evil.*" (Proverbs 16:6 NKJV)
- "*By humility and the fear of the LORD, are riches and honor and life.*" (Proverbs 22:4 NKJV)
- "*Do not let your heart envy sinners but be zealous for the fear of the LORD all day.*" (Proverbs 23:17 NKJV)
- "*Wisdom and knowledge will be the stability of your times, and the strength of salvation; the fear of the LORD is His treasure.*" (Isaiah 33:6 NKJV)

- *"And walking in the fear of the Lord and in the comfort of the Holy Spirit, they were multiplied."* (Acts 9:31 NKJV)
- *"Who is the man that fears the LORD? Him shall He teach in the way He chooses. He himself shall dwell in prosperity, And his descendants shall inherit the earth. The secret of the LORD is with those who fear Him, And He will show them His covenant."* (Psalm 25:12–14 NKJV)

It is better to have little and trust in the Lord than to have many earthly possessions without the Lord. It is better to be with the Lord, period, *"Better is a little with the fear of the LORD, than great treasure with trouble."* (Proverbs 15:16 NKJV)

There is a whole Psalm dedicated to the man who fears the Lord, *"Praise the LORD! Blessed is the man who fears the LORD, who delights greatly in His commandments."* (Psalm 112:1 NKJV) The remainder of the Psalms goes on to tell of all the blessings for the one who fears the Lord. It includes that His descendants will be mighty on the earth, he will have riches and wealth, will not be afraid of evil, and his heart is steadfast trusting in the Lord. One is wise to fear the Lord.

Fear embodies the tension between grace and truth. It captures the difficulty in relating to God. God has provided us fear. In that, He has provided an emotion that runs the gamut. From the awe of who He is as a loving Father to the fear of who He is as the Holy and Righteous Judge. *"For God has not given us a spirit of fear, but of power and of love and of a sound mind."* (2 Timothy 1:7 NKJV) But we need to stay humble and *"work out your own salvation with fear and trembling."* (Philippians 2:12b NKJV)

Pray that when we find that Jesus is enough and God is a loving Father, and with the help of the Spirit we will be able to say, *"The LORD is my helper; I will not fear. What can man do to me?"* (Hebrews 13:6b NKJV)

Devotional – Cops

When I was younger, we used to always point out the cops. It was like we were doing something bad or we were always worried that we would get in trouble. And then when we would call out that there was a cop in the area, we would all straighten up and act right. As soon as it was clear, then back to being knuckleheads. Then there came a time when I realized that there was nothing to be afraid of with the cops around. I preferred that they were around. I didn't have anything to fear. They were there to protect me. I used to treat God the same way. I feared Him. And not the awe kind of fear. It was that I was scared that He would punish me. Wasn't sure I wanted Him around unless I was in trouble and needed His help. And then I would come running back to Him on my knees in prayer. So, just like the cops, there came a time when I no longer feared God in the way that I was scared of Him, but I feared Him in that I was in awe of Him. I wanted to be in His presence. I felt safe with Him in my life. Even better was to have Him run my life.

CHAPTER 9

YIELDING TO THE HOLY SPIRIT

"And I (Jesus) will pray the Father, and He will give you another Helper, that He may abide with you forever—the Spirit of truth, whom the world cannot receive, because it neither sees Him nor knows Him; but you know Him, for He dwells with you and will be in you."

(JOHN 14:16–17 NKJV)

Christianity is hard because we must give up control. The Holy Spirit will not force himself on us. He won't force us to learn. He won't force us to accept Christ. We must be willing to yield. We must choose to yield to the Holy Spirit. We need to submit to His wisdom and leadership. It is unique and counterculture in our world to willfully submit to His lead. We can only be led if we are willing to follow, *"For as many as are led by the Spirit of God, these are sons of God."* (Romans 8:4 NKJV)

The Spirit wants us to submit to God. To yield to His will, *"Or do you think that the Scripture says in vain, 'The Spirit who dwells in us yearns jealously'? But He gives more grace. Therefore, He says: 'God resists the proud, but gives grace to the humble.' Therefore, submit to God. Resist the devil and he will flee from you."* (James 4:5–7 NKJV) Submitting to God is key to the spiritual warfare that plaques us daily. Yielding to the Holy

Spirit unleashes His power to work in and through us, *"You shall receive power when the Holy Spirit has come upon you; and you shall be witnesses to Me in Jerusalem, and in all Judea and Samaria, and to the end of the earth."* (Acts 1:8 NKJV)

It is wise to yield, *"But the wisdom that is from above is first pure, then peaceable, gentle, willing to yield, full of mercy and good fruits, without partiality and without hypocrisy."* (James 3:17 NKJV)

Giving up control is very hard for some people to do. In fact, some never get past it. The concept of presenting ourselves to be led involves a willingness to follow. This means that we give up our own will and submit to God's will. *"Do you not know that to whom you present yourselves slaves to obey, you are that one's slaves whom you obey, whether of sin leading to death, or of obedience leading to righteousness?"* (Romans 6:16 NKJV) To whom will we yield, *"And do not present your members as instruments of unrighteousness to sin but present yourselves to God as being alive from the dead, and your members as instruments of righteousness to God."* (Romans 6:13 NKJV)

The world doesn't know the Spirit because they haven't accepted Jesus as their Savior and Lord. Even though the Spirit is working on them and trying to bring them to Christ. The world still doesn't realize that it is the Spirit of God presenting the truth to them. Jesus gives us the Holy Spirit when we are born again, *"And I will pray the Father, and He will give you another Helper, that He may abide with you forever—the Spirit of truth, whom the world cannot receive, because it neither sees Him nor knows Him; but you know Him, for He dwells with you and will be in you."* (John 14:16–17 NKJV) The Spirit is our Helper.

The Holy Spirit convicts us of our need for a Savior. He shows us Christ, *"And when He (The Holy Spirit) has come, He will convict the world of sin, and of righteousness, and of judgment: of sin, because they do not believe in Me."* (John 16:8–9 NKJV) Watching the Holy Spirit work on bringing folks to the Lord shows that He is at work in every nonbeliever. We can watch Him work on someone's heart, pointing them toward Jesus Christ. It is wonderful and encouraging to witness, *"But God has revealed them to us through His Spirit. For the Spirit searches all things, yes, the deep things of God."* (1 Corinthians 2:10 NKJV) The nonbeliever, most times, is fighting the Spirit, wrestling to believe. They are trying to know. Yet the Spirit is patient and persistent, waiting for the person to yield. He reveals the knowledge of God and Jesus to all. The Spirit continues to testify of Jesus, *"The Spirit of truth who proceeds from the Father, He will testify of Me."* (John 15:26b NKJV)

Christianity is hard because we try in vain to understand God without the help of the Holy Spirit. We must acknowledge that without God and His helper, we are hopelessly lost. *"His ways are past finding out."* (Romans 11:33b NKJV) This is the conclusion that Job discovers after many arguments with his friends and being questioned by God. *"Then Job answered the LORD and said: 'I know that You can do everything, and that no purpose of Yours can be withheld from You. You asked, "Who is this who hides counsel without knowledge?" Therefore, I have uttered what I did not understand, things too wonderful for me, which I did not know.'"* (Job 42:1–3 NKJV)

The Holy Spirit will present the truth to the believer and nonbeliever equally. The believer grabs hold of the truth and acts on it. The nonbeliever resists the truth. The Holy Spirit will help us and guide us into the truth, *"But the Helper, the Holy Spirit, whom the Father will send in My name, He will teach you all things, and bring to your remembrance all things that I said to you."* (John 14:26 NKJV) We receive the Spirit through faith *"that we might receive the promise of the Spirit through faith."* (Galatians 3:14b NKJV) For those who continue to resist the truth, the Spirit will let us have our way, *"And the LORD said, 'My Spirit shall not strive with man forever, for he is indeed flesh.'"* (Genesis 6:3a NKJV)

The Holy Spirit lives inside every believer. Jesus provides the Holy Spirit to be with us in His absence. The Holy Spirit is our companion through the faith journey. He is our teacher, helper, and guide. He is provided to us to further the relationship with God the Father and Jesus the Son. This verse depicts the interrelationship of the Trinity and their relationship to us, *"The grace of the Lord Jesus Christ, and the love of God, and the communion of the Holy Spirit be with you all.*" (2 Corinthians 13:14 NKJV) Communion means to be a partner, companion, or associate.

Christianity is hard because the Holy Spirit will let us be us. He gives us the freedom to choose. He doesn't force Himself on us and is willing to let us live with the consequences of our actions. He will leave us to our own devices if we choose. We must let Him have control of us. The Holy Spirit is key to growing your faith. The Holy Spirit is a member of the Trinity, having all the attributes of God.

Even though the Holy Spirit will let us have our will and way, it doesn't mean that He still can't grieve over our choices. The Holy Spirit loves us and wants the best for us. He knows what we can be and the life we were meant to live. When we don't willingly accept His leadership and follow Him, it grieves Him, "*And do not grieve the Holy Spirit of God, by whom you were sealed for the day of redemption. Let all bitterness, wrath, anger, clamor, and evil speaking be put away from you, with all malice. And be kind to one another, tenderhearted, forgiving one another, even as God in Christ forgave you.*" (Ephesians 4:30–32 NKJV)

Christianity is hard because we must live in the Spirit, not the flesh. This isn't natural for us as we were born with a sinful nature. We must be born of the Spirit to experience the things of the Spirit. If we haven't been reborn into the Spirit, we can't understand the things of the Spirit, "*Jesus answered, 'Most assuredly, I say to you, unless one is born of water and the Spirit, he cannot enter the kingdom of God. That which is born of the flesh is flesh, and that which is born of the Spirit is spirit.*'" (John 3:5–8 NKJV)

The Bible summarizes the relationship with the Spirit and the need for every believer to live in the Spirit, "*There is therefore now no condemnation to those who are in Christ Jesus, who do not walk according to the flesh, but according to the Spirit. For the law of the Spirit of life in Christ Jesus has made me free from the law of sin and death. For what the law could not do in that it was weak through the flesh, God did by sending His own Son in the likeness of sinful flesh, on account of sin: He condemned sin in the flesh, that the righteous requirement of the law might be fulfilled in us who do not walk according to the flesh but according to the Spirit. For those who live according to the flesh set their minds on the things of the flesh, but those who live according to the Spirit, the things of the Spirit. For to be carnally minded is death, but to be spiritually minded is life and peace. Because the carnal mind is enmity against God; for it is not subject to the law of God, nor indeed can be. So then, those who are in the flesh cannot please God. But you are not in the flesh but in the Spirit, if indeed the Spirit of God dwells in you. Now if anyone does not have the Spirit of Christ, he is not His.*" (Romans 8:1–9 NKJV)

We are presented with the choice whether to live by the Spirit or live by our own flesh. Disciples are to live by the Spirit. There are both eternal and temporal consequences to this choice, "*For if you live according to the flesh you will die; but if by the Spirit you put to death the deeds of the body, you will live.*" (Romans 8:13 NKJV) While the choice to not follow the Spirit may make sense to the unbeliever, the result is known, "*For he who sows to his flesh will of the flesh reap corruption, but he who sows to the Spirit will of the Spirit reap everlasting life.*" (Galatians 6:8 NKJV) Make a wise choice today.

Christianity is hard because the spiritual world is real. Many don't recognize this fact, and even if they do, they are ill-prepared to deal with it. It is only though the Spirit of God that we can entertain any ability to operate or live in this world. The Spirit of God will lead us to victory if we let Him.

In the spiritual world, there are many spirits. We are to test the spirits to know whether they are of God or not, "*Beloved, do not believe every spirit, but test the spirits, whether they are of God; because many false prophets have gone out into the world. By this you know the Spirit of God: Every spirit that confesses that Jesus Christ has come in the flesh is of God, and every spirit that does not confess that Jesus Christ has come in the flesh is not of God. And this is the spirit of the Antichrist, which you have heard was coming, and is now already in the world.*" (1 John 4:1–3 NKJV)

There are many examples in the Bible about spirits who were living inside people. Here are just two examples. First is two demons block-ing a passage that took up residence in two men, "*When He (Jesus) had come to the other side, to the country of the Gergesenes, there met Him two demon-possessed men, coming out of the tombs, exceedingly fierce, so that no one could pass that way. And suddenly they cried out, saying, 'What have we to do with You, Jesus, You Son of God? Have You come here to torment us before the time?'"* (Matthew 8:28–29 NKJV) Jesus grants the wish of the demon to be expelled into a herd of swine. The second example is of Jesus healing a young mute boy, *"And He was casting out a demon, and it was mute. So, it was, when the demon had gone out, that the mute spoke; and the multitudes marveled."* (Luke 11:14 NKJV)

Please don't underestimate the influence of evil spirits. The evil spirits will take up residence and control us. They control many in our world. Without the Holy Spirit, it is worthless to try and rid the evil spirits on our own, *"When an unclean spirit goes out of a man, he goes through dry places, seeking rest, and finds none. Then he says, 'I will return to my house from which I came.' And when he comes, he finds it empty, swept, and put in order. Then he goes and takes with him seven other spirits more wicked than himself, and they enter and dwell there; and the last state of that man is worse than the first. So, shall it also be with this wicked generation."* (Matthew 12:43–45 NKJV)

If we are to understand the spiritual world, then we need to look at both sides. People many times only look at Christianity and point out all its flaws. How hard it is to follow. How awful Christians act. How can a loving Father, God, allow all the evil in the world? What very rarely enters the decision-making process is Satan's role. He is a liar. He deceives. His way leads to destruction. Here is what Jesus says to the Pharisees, *"You are of your father the devil, and the desires of your father you want to do. He was a murderer from the beginning, and does not stand in the truth, because there is no truth in him. When he speaks a lie, he speaks from his own resources, for he is a liar and the father of it"* John 8:44 (NKJV) When people truly evaluate both sides of the decision, the choice is clear. The decision is easier to make when both sides of the choice are understood. When people choose Satan and his lies, they will live with the consequences.

Christianity is hard because we don't question Satan's lies like we question God's love. Satan will draw many away with his lies, *"Now the Spirit expressly says that in latter times some will depart from the faith, giving heed to deceiving spirits and doctrines of demons."* (1 Timothy 4:1 NKJV) Whom will we believe?

People often blame God for all of Satan's actions. When we believe the lies of Satan, then we end up walking in the destruction brought on by Satan, *"in which you once walked according to the course of this world, according to the prince of the power of the air, the spirit who now works in the sons of disobedience."* (Ephesians 2:2 NKJV) But for some reason (see chapter on Choice), God is letting Satan rule on this earth.

Christianity is hard because of the mysteries of God. It is the Spirit who teaches us the mysteries of God. We need to yield to the Spirit to understand these mysteries, which is a mystery in and of itself, *"But as it is written: "Eye has not seen, nor ear heard, nor have entered into the heart of man the things which God has prepared for those who love Him." But God has revealed them to us through His Spirit. For the Spirit searches all things, yes, the deep things of God."* (1Cor 6: 9–10 NKJV)

We are not only taught by the Holy Spirit, but He also wants us to share that knowledge with others, *"Go therefore and make disciples of all the nations, baptizing them in the name of the Father and of the Son and of the Holy Spirit, teaching them to observe all things that I have commanded you; and lo, I am with you always, even to the end of the age."* (Matthew 28:18–20 NKJV)

Christianity is hard because we try to live the Christian life by ourselves. Yielding to the Holy Spirit and all His power (omnipresence, omniscience, and omnipotence) makes living the Christian life possible.

The Holy Spirit is omnipresent (always present). The Spirit always seems to be around. He was there at creation, *"The earth was without form, and void; and darkness was on the face of the deep. And the Spirit of God was hovering over the face of the waters."* (Genesis 1:2 NKJV) He was with David, *"Then Samuel took the horn of oil and anointed him in the midst of his brothers; and the Spirit of the LORD came upon David from that day forward.*" (1 Samuel 16:13 NKJV) He was there at the baptism of Jesus, "*And immediately, coming up from the water, He saw the heavens parting and the Spirit descending upon Him like a dove.*" (Mark 1:10 NKJV) The Spirit is everywhere, "*Where can I go from Your Spirit? Or where can I flee from Your presence? If I ascend into heaven, you are there; If I make my bed in hell, behold, you are there.*" (Psalm 139:7–8 NKJV) He will be there at the end encouraging everyone to drink of the river of water of life, "*And the Spirit and the bride say, 'Come!' And let him who hears say, 'Come!' And let him who thirsts come. Whoever desires, let him take the water of life freely.*" (Revelation 22:17 NKJV) The Holy Spirit is going to be there for us. Do we believe it?

The Holy Spirit is omniscient (all-knowing). The only way to know the things of God is through the Spirit of God. The Holy Spirit teaches us all things. He teaches us the spiritual things of God. He reveals to us the things which God has prepared for those who love Him, "*But God has revealed them to us through His Spirit. For the Spirit searches all things, yes, the deep things of God. For what man knows the things of a man except the spirit of the man which is in him? Even so no one knows the things of God except the Spirit of God. Now we have received, not the spirit of the world, but the Spirit who is from God, that we might know the things that have been freely given to us by God. These things we also speak, not in words which man's wisdom teaches but which the Holy Spirit teaches, comparing spiritual things with spiritual.*" (1 Corinthians 2:9–13 NKJV)

The Holy Spirit is omnipotent (all-powerful). The apostle Paul used the power of the Holy Spirit to spread the good news of Jesus Christ "*in mighty signs and wonders, by the power of the Spirit of God, so that from Jerusalem and round about to Illyricum I have fully preached the gospel of Christ Romans.*" (Romans 15:19 NKJV) And again in Corinthians, Paul states that his preaching wasn't of his own doing, but the power of the Spirit, "*And my speech and my preaching were not with persuasive words of human wisdom, but in demonstration of the Spirit and of power, that your faith should not be in the wisdom of men but in the power of God.*" (1

Corinthians 2:4–5 NKJV) The Spirit's power guarded and protected Jesus during His ministry here on earth, "*Then Jesus returned in the power of the Spirit to Galilee, and news of Him went out through all the surrounding region.*" (Luke 4:14 NKJV)

The Holy Spirit inspired the writing of the Bible, "*Knowing this first, that no prophecy of Scripture is of any private interpretation, for prophecy never came by the will of man, but holy men of God spoke as they were moved by the Holy Spirit.*" (2 Peter 1:20–21 NKJV)

The Holy Spirit is eternal. The Spirit is life. The Spirit gives us life because the Spirit is life. Sin and the flesh lead to death. We were dead in our sins. This bible passage describes how much the Spirit brings us into the life of Christ, "*And if Christ is in you, the body is dead because of sin, but the Spirit is life because of righteousness. But if the Spirit of Him who raised Jesus from the dead dwells in you, He who raised Christ from the dead will also give life to your mortal bodies through His Spirit who dwells in you. Therefore, brethren, we are debtors—not to the flesh, to live according to the flesh. For if you live according to the flesh you will die; but if by the Spirit you put to death the deeds of the body, you will live. For as many as are led by the Spirit of God, these are sons of God. For you did not receive the spirit of bondage again to fear, but you received the Spirit of adoption by whom we cry out, 'Abba, Father.' The Spirit Himself bears witness with our spirit that we are children of God, and if children, then heirs—heirs of God and joint heirs with Christ, if indeed we suffer with Him, that we may also be glorified together.*" (Romans 8:10–17 NKJV)

Christianity is hard because we quench the Spirit often. The Bible instructs us, "*Do not quench the Spirit.*" (1 Thessalonians 5:19 NKJV) Often the Spirit is at work in our lives and then we take control. We think we know better. Even after the prodding of the Holy Spirit, we will take matters into our own hands. We end up getting in the way and trying to do things ourselves. The Spirit will let us go and not take control. We must willingly give the Spirit control. If we try to keep control, then that grieves the Holy Spirit. It makes Him sad when He lets us destroy our lives because of our unwillingness to follow Him.

To whom will we yield? Do we follow Satan, or do we follow God? This is a day in, day out choice. It is a hard concept for us to understand: to give up our will. We say to ourselves we must be able to do something. How do we let the Spirit of God lead us? This is where the Spirit of God enables us. We must be attuned to the Spirit so we can follow His lead. *"I beseech you therefore, brethren, by the mercies of God, that you present your bodies a living sacrifice, holy, acceptable to God, which is your reasonable service. And do not be conformed to this world, but be transformed by the renewing of your mind, that you may prove what is that good and acceptable and perfect will of God."* (Romans 12:1–2 NKJV) The choice to present our bodies is a conscience choice that says, "Here we are, use us".

Here is an example from the Old testament that shows the children of Israel how to choose God. Yield ourselves to the Lord and he will not turn His face from us, *"Now do not be stiff-necked, as your fathers were, but yield yourselves to the LORD; and enter His sanctuary, which He has sanctified forever, and serve the LORD your God, that the fierceness of His wrath may turn away from you. For if you return to the LORD, your brethren and your children will be treated with compassion by those who lead them captive, so that they may come back to this land; for the LORD your God is gracious and merciful, and will not turn His face from you if you return to Him."* (2 Chronicles 30:8–9 NKJV)

When we are yielded to the Spirit and act in accordance with His instructions, then the fruits of the Spirit appear in our life, *"For you were once darkness, but now you are light in the Lord. Walk as children of light (for the fruit of the Spirit is in all goodness, righteousness, and truth), finding out what is acceptable to the Lord."* (Ephesians 5:8–10 NKJV) The Spirit equips us with gifts and talents. When we follow the Spirit and yield to Him, then our life produces the fruit.

Our bodies are now the temple of God, *"Do you not know that you are the temple of God and that the Spirit of God dwells in you?"* (1 Corinthians 3:16 NKJV) This has many positive implications that can relate back to the Old Testament and the history of the temple. The temple was the place to worship God. It was the holy place where God would reside with His people. We are the temple of God; He lives inside of us. He knows everything about us.

In the Old Testament, before Jesus' Ministry on earth, the Spirit was provided on an as-needed case to fulfill God's will and purpose. God would provide the Holy Spirit in specific situations. The Spirit was prophesized to provide life and the knowledge of the Lord, "*I will put My Spirit in you, and you shall live, and I will place you in your own land. Then you shall know that I, the LORD, have spoken it and performed it," says the LORD.*'" (Ezekiel 37:14 NKJV) The Spirit was provided by filling the person by the concept of pouring, "*And I will pour on the house of David and on the inhabitants of Jerusalem the Spirit of grace and supplication; then they will look on Me whom they pierced. Yes, they will mourn for Him as one mourns for his only son and grieve for Him as one grieves for a first-born.*" (Zechariah 12:10 NKJV) "*I will pour out My Spirit in those days.*" (Joel 2:29b NKJV)

The Holy Spirit came upon folks to fulfill God's purpose. Here are few examples, "*The Spirit of the LORD came upon him* (Othniel), *and he judged Israel.*" (Judges 3:10a NKJV) And for Gideon, "*the Spirit of the LORD came upon Gideon; then he blew the trumpet, and the Abiezrites gathered behind him.*" (Judges 6:34). And on David's deathbed, the Spirit spoke through David, "*The Spirit of the LORD spoke by me, And His word was on my tongue.*" (2 Samuel 23:2 NKJV)

When the Spirit came upon people, He changed them, "*Then the Spirit of the LORD will come upon you, and you will prophesy with them and be turned into another man.*" (1 Samuel 10:6 NKJV) The Holy Spirit wants to help us to become the person God meant for us to be. God has a plan and purpose for our life, believe it.

After Jesus' ministry, we are given the Spirit full-time to live within us. We have the power of the Holy Spirit within us. The Holy Spirit is a gift from God to those who have accepted Jesus Christ as their Savior, "*The Holy Spirit fell upon all those who heard the word. And those of the circumcision who believed were astonished, as many as came with Peter, because the gift of the Holy Spirit had been poured out on the Gentiles also."* (Acts 10:44 NKJV)

Once received, the Holy Spirit seals us with a blessed assurance of our salvation, *"In Him you also trusted, after you heard the word of truth, the gospel of your salvation; in whom also, having believed, you were sealed with the Holy Spirit of promise."* (Ephesians 1:13 NKJV) God is able. Do we believe it?

Pray that we give up control and yield to the Holy Spirit to guide our life.

CHAPTER 10

LOVING OTHERS

"And if there is any other commandment, are all summed up in this saying, namely, "You shall love your neighbor as yourself."

(ROMANS 13:9B NKJV)

C hristianity is hard because some people are difficult to love. God commands us to love others, *"A new commandment I give to you, that you love one another."* (Jn 13:34a NKJV) As if that wasn't going to be hard enough, God adds this additional standard, *"As I have loved you, that you also love one another."* (Jn 13:34b NKJV) Loving others as God loved them seems like a pretty high standard. It is very difficult to love some of the people on this earth. Some people are easy to love and others are difficult to love.

God sets the standard for us to follow. God also uses the love of others as a standard to be His disciple, *"By this all will know that you are My disciples, if you have love for one another."* (Jn 13:35 NKJV) And others includes our enemies, *"But I say to you who hear: Love your enemies, do good to those who hate you, bless those who curse you, and pray for those who spitefully use you."* (Luke 6:27–28 NKJV)

We need to provide to others the same love and grace that is given freely to us. We are not naturally people of grace. Humans can be so cruel to each other. It is not in our nature to forgive people or give them something they haven't earned or deserve. Accounts of this cruelty are well documented in the Bible. Starting with Cain and Abel after the fall of man. Joseph was sold by his brothers into slavery. King Saul tried multiple times to kill David. David's own son tried to kill him. David had Uriah killed by sending him to the front lines of the battle. And yet we are supposed to love these people.

Those are all Old Testament accounts. Let's look at what happened to Paul as he spread the good news of the Gospel, "*From the Jews five times I received forty stripes minus one. Three times I was beaten with rods; once I was stoned; three times I was shipwrecked; a night and a day I have been in the deep; in journeys often, in perils of waters, in perils of robbers, in perils of my own countrymen, in perils of the Gentiles, in perils in the city, in perils in the wilderness, in perils in the sea, in perils among false brethren; in weariness and toil, in sleeplessness often, in hunger and thirst, in fastings often, in cold and nakedness.*" (2 Corinthians 11:24–27 NKJV)

Paul understood the depravity of man and how hard it is to be a Christian. He had experienced it. Even with all that, he ends this passage with a concern (love) for people, "*Besides the other things, what comes upon me daily: my deep concern for all the churches.*" (2 Corinthians 11:28 NKJV) That can only be done through the power of Jesus Christ.

We could spend much of this chapter talking about dealing with all the oddities of the human mind and spirit. It is important to focus on Christ as the answer to loving others. It is through Jesus that we have the power and wisdom to see people as He sees them. We all have a distinct desire within us to be loved and accepted. God created us to love and be loved. Most, if not all, of people's actions are driven by a need for acceptance and love.

Christianity is hard because God commands us to love all people. There must be a way to love and accept people whom God loves. The kind who cross our paths and are difficult to love or even like. A couple of key points to remember when dealing with this situation. First is that we all have sin in our lives. What makes us think we are better than anyone else?

Therefore, we should have compassion on this individual. Second point is that we should be ready to give a reason for the hope that is in us. Most of the folks in this situation need hope. We can love on them but by providing hope, we can help them see themselves as God's child. Third point is the person's heart. Is that person seeking forgiveness and repentance? If that person is just looking for someone to say it is ok for them to continue to sin, then we are doing that person a disservice by condoning their sin. They need to be looking for help and we should show them love. If they aren't looking for help, then we should still love them by showing them the consequences of their actions. This may take a long time.

Love never fails. (1Cor 3:8 NKJV) It may take a long time. Love is a choice. Continue to make a conscious choice to love someone and believe the fact that love will never fail. This also makes Christianity hard when we don't see the results of love right away.

Personal application – Christianity is hard because we are to love others as yourself, "*and if there is any other commandment, are all summed up in this saying, namely, 'You shall love your neighbor as yourself.'*" (Romans 13:9b NKJV) I have always taken this to mean that I need to treat others with the utmost love and respect. Until one day, I thought of how I treat myself. I am hard on myself. If I am to love my neighbor as myself, then I must consider how I do love myself.

Here are some of the ways I love myself. I will take care of myself at the end of the day. I won't hurt myself. I make sure I have all the basics in life to survive. This passage represents what the Lord means when we are to love others, "*For I was hungry and you gave Me food; I was thirsty and you gave Me drink; I was a stranger and you took Me in; I was naked and you clothed Me; I was sick and you visited Me; I was in prison and you came to Me.*" (Matthew 25:35–36 NKJV)

Tough love often doesn't come across as very loving. Once the basic needs are met, I will also hold myself accountable. I expect more from myself than others, therefore I have trouble forgiving myself. I am often disappointed in myself. Is this the way I am supposed to love others, because that is the way I love myself? If I don't love myself, how can I love others?

Forgiveness comes fairly easy for me when I am forgiving others. But forgiving myself is very difficult for me. I have higher expectations of myself, therefore forgiving myself is difficult. So, if I was to treat others as myself, then I would have difficulty forgiving others, *"And be kind to one another, tenderhearted, forgiving one another, even as God in Christ forgave you."* (Eph 4:32 NKJV) I pray that the Father will give me the strength and wisdom to forgive others and myself as I have been forgiven.

I will discipline myself. The Lord disciplines those He loves, *"For whom the LORD loves He chastens, And scourges every son whom He receives."* (Hebrews 12:6 NKJV) If we want the best for those we love, then we should hold them accountable for their actions. Jesus held folks accountable. He was tough on the rich young ruler (Luke 18:22 NKJV), pharisees (Matt 23:13 NKJV) and future disciples (Luke 14:26–27 NKJV). And then there is this instruction of how to deal with someone living in sin, *"In the name of our Lord Jesus Christ, when you are gathered together, along with my spirit, with the power of our Lord Jesus Christ, deliver such a one to Satan for the destruction of the flesh, that his spirit may be saved in the day of the Lord Jesus."* (1 Corinthians 5:4–5 NKJV) That is some tough love right there.

People are going to make us mad. They are not perfect. They are going to make mistakes. We can't let this get in our way. We need to love those people and help them through their unbelief. To love people, we need to forgive them.

Don't let the action of others keep us from believing in God. There is a mindset out there that says: if God is all-powerful and all-loving, how can His people be so hateful? Christians ought not to act that way. So if

His people act that way, then He must not be real. Otherwise, He would fix it. It is important to understand that we are all broken. The relationship is between God and us individually. There are many who call themselves Christians who aren't following Jesus. While other Christians are in various states of spiritual maturity. We shouldn't use them as a reason not to have our own relationship with Christ. We shouldn't let others affect our relationship with God. This is difficult and hard to do.

Love is a choice. We can choose to love others or not. God desires for us to choose to love others. God loves us enough to let us choose. We demand the choice, but then we expect Jesus to fix it when we screw it up (see chapter on Choice). And God is trying to fix it one heart at a time, *"Then I will give them a heart to know Me, that I am the LORD; and they shall be My people, and I will be their God, for they shall return to Me with their whole heart."* (Jeremiah 24:7 NKJV) Pray that we will let Him fix ours today. Especially the one who is keeping us from having a relationship with God.

A key to loving others is to believe and experience that Jesus is enough. Jesus made everything. Jesus is everything, *"All things were made through Him, and without Him nothing was made that was made."* (John 1:3 NKJV) And life is found through Jesus Christ, *"In Him was life, and the life was the light of men."* (John 1:4 NKJV)

This is a repeat from the chapter on Jesus, but worth repeating here. Through Jesus we have everything. Through Jesus Christ our Lord we have faith (Acts 15:11 NKJV), redemption (Rom 3:24 NKJV), love (Titus 3:4–6 NKJV), peace (Rom 5:1, Phil 4:7 NKJV), reconciliation (Rom 5:11 NKJV), righteousness (Rom 5:17 NKJV), new life (1Cor 8:6 NKJV), victory (1Cor 15:57 NKJV), triumph (2Cor 2:14 NKJV), trust (2Cor 3:4 NKJV), salvation (1Th 5:9 NKJV), wise (2Tim 3:15 NKJV), complete (Heb 13:21 NKJV), hope (1Pet 1:3 NKJV), grace (Jn 1:17 NKJV), truth (Jn 1:17 NKJV), and all things (1Cor 8:6, Eph 3:9 NKJV). We are rich (2Cor 8:9 NKJV), a child of God (Gal 3:26 NKJV), and an heir (Gal 4:7 NKJV). Jesus is the way, the truth, and the life (Jn 14:6 NKJV) Let the word of God sink deep into our heart that Jesus is enough.

Through Christ all things are possible, *"Jesus said to him, "If you can believe, all things are possible to him who believes."* (Mark 9:23 NKJV) God is able. Do we believe it?

When Jesus is enough, then we aren't placing our needs on others. We aren't looking for them to fill a hole in our life. This is especially important in a marriage. If we are looking for our spouse to fill certain needs in our life, we will eventually be sorely disappointed. Jesus will never disappoint us. He is enough.

Once we quit having expectations from other people, then it frees us to see them how Jesus sees them. When someone makes our blood boil (that means to make us mad), then try and look at them like Jesus looks at them. Jesus loves them. Yes, believe it or not, Jesus loves that person who persecutes, bullies, harasses, destroys, and otherwise ruins our life. Bullies are really acting out of a need for love and attention. They think the only way to be noticed is to act out. Under the hard shell of a bully is a scared person screaming out for love. Jesus desires all, even bullies, to come to a saving knowledge of Himself. (1 Tim 2:4 NKJV) Jesus died for them too. When we are focused on Jesus and His relationship with us, then our relationship with others will pale in comparison. We can start to mimic that relationship in all our other relationships. Jesus will supply all our needs, *"And my God shall supply all your need according to His riches in glory by Christ Jesus."* (Philippians 4:19 NKJV) This includes our need of the ability to love difficult people. There isn't a reason to look anywhere else to have our needs met. Pray and ask for God's provision today.

Christianity is hard because of the amount of grace that we need and use. At one of the churches we attended, the staff and leadership would define some of the congregation as Extra Grace Required (EGRs). These are the people who require extra grace when dealing with them. There are some people who are just difficult. Others are just annoying. Yet still, some are just mean. This makes Christianity especially hard as we expect more from Christians. But they are just people too. There are many Christians at different levels of maturity and faith, making it difficult to hold them accountable. We must show them grace. And yet we are to love them.

Personal application – As I was starting to use the term EGR, God reminded me that I am an EGR. I have clearly used my share of grace. And will still need more. Since I am the recipient of a lot of grace, then I ought to show grace to others.

When we realize that we are an EGR and deserve nothing more, then it helps us look at people differently. Especially when we think we are all that, how much more grace do we require? Everyone is valuable to the Lord and so it shall be with us also. We are all EGRs and the more grace and love we can show each other will go a long way to helping everyone's joy to increase, including our own.

Thankfully and hopefully to increase everyone's joy, the Bible gives instructions on dealing with others in Philippians, "*Fulfill my joy by being like-minded, having the same love, being of one accord, of one mind. Let nothing be done through selfish ambition or conceit, but in lowliness of mind let each esteem others better than himself. Let each of you look out not only for his own interests, but also for the interests of others.*" (Philippians 2:2–4 NKJV)

When we are looking out for number one (ourselves), we lose the ability to see others as God sees them. Putting others down doesn't raise us up. It only denigrates someone who the Lord loves. Please remember who gives us our life, abilities, gifts, and resources. It all comes from God.

It is only through and by the grace of God that we can do anything. "*For by grace you have been saved through faith, and that not of yourselves; it is the gift of God.*" (Ephesians 2:8 NKJV) Thank God for His unlimited provision of grace to us. We seem to need more every day. Especially as the Spirit of God reveals more sin in our life. We are truly an extra grace required. Grace, grace, and more grace—it seems that we can't get enough grace. How wonderful grace is to the woeful sinner such as we are, "*And of His fullness we have all received, and grace for grace.*" (John 1:16 NKJV)

Christianity is hard because His church is full of redeemed sinners trying to figure it out. If we go to church for any other reason than to glorify God, we will be disappointed. Everyone has disappointed someone at some point in their spiritual walk. Quit looking to others for your spiritual welfare.

Christianity is hard because Christians will disappoint us. Churches have placed pastors on a pedestal and called the head of the church. This is an unreasonable expectation. The church members are placing too much on a man. He will disappoint us. The only head of the church is Jesus Christ. If we get that wrong, then we will bring discord and disruption to the church body. Jesus Christ is the head of the church. (Col 1:18 NKJV) Pastors will sin and the church will experience discord and disruption. It will tear the body apart. Satan is able to sow discord because the focus of the people was on a man instead of Jesus Christ.

This verse is used to encourage folks to attend church, "*not forsaking the assembling of ourselves together, as is the manner of some, but exhorting one another, and so much the more as you see the Day approaching.*" (Hebrews 10:25 NKJV) Most folks focus on the assembly of ourselves. It is the exhorting others that is the key action. Let's not be a stumbling block to others. Let's help them glorify God. And in that process, we learn to love them.

When we go to church to glorify God, then God will be honored in all our actions. We will be focused on Him and all the other actions will be put in the proper perspective. When our focus is on honoring and glorifying God, then if the pastor doesn't hit a home run with the sermon, or the music wasn't to our liking, we can praise God that others are worshiping God in their own way. We will have more compassion and consideration of others in their way of expressing their love of God. We can only control our actions. Glorify God with our actions.

It is very hard to love someone we don't respect. Respect must come first. As Paul gives instructions in Ephesians about husbands loving their wives, he doesn't tell the wives to love their husbands. He tells them to respect them, "*Let the wife see that she respects her husband.*" (Ephesians 5:33b NKJV)

We should love others enough to not let them go to hell. When confronted with many of the expectations of today's society to be tolerant, we need to realize that the tolerance they are requesting or even requiring will lead them straight to hell. We need to share the love of Christ and His message of redemption. Pray for wisdom. We often don't share the Gospel because we are worried about pleasing man as opposed to pleasing God. Pray for the courage to share Him with other people, "*Pursue peace with all people, and holiness, without which no one will see the Lord: looking carefully lest anyone fall short of the grace of God; lest any root of bitterness springing up cause trouble, and by this many become defiled.*" (Hebrews 12:14–15 NKJV)

Loving others is difficult at best. Only through the belief that Jesus is enough can we love others the way God intended. Through Jesus we can love others. When we reflect His love for others, we can love them even in the most difficult of times.

CHAPTER 11

LIVING IN ANTICIPATION (PRAYER)

"Let us therefore come boldly to the throne of grace, that we may obtain mercy and find grace to help in time of need."

(HEBREWS 4:16 NKJV)

C hristianity is hard because prayer takes faith. Praying is talking to God. Prayer acknowledges God and our need of Him. Prayer is a confession of faith. By praying we are saying that we believe in God. God is going to answer the prayer, so we ought to just live in anticipation of the answer. Do you believe it?

Praying brings peace to the soul. It gives us hope. Praying helps us in our time of need, *"Let us therefore come boldly to the throne of grace, that we may obtain mercy and find grace to help in time of need."* (Hebrews 4:16 NKJV) It is a privilege to be able to pray to God through His Son Jesus Christ and with the help of the Holy Spirit.

We ought to pray all the time and at any time. God is with us all the time. We can just start up a conversation and He hears us. The situation doesn't matter. We can pray in meetings, while eating, socializing, during a verbal disagreement (especially good time to pray), driving (keep your eyes open and pay attention to the road), during times of stress and times of joy. People don't need to know that we are praying. We can talk to God without any outward signs. This is just between God and us.

Christianity is hard because prayers aren't always answered the way we want. We tend to look for the answer to be a specific outcome. When the prayer is answered differently, it is hard to realize that it was the answer. God answers the prayer, nonetheless. We need to pay attention and look for the answer to prayer. The answer may not be immediate. It may not be the answer we wanted. It may not even be in our timing. There are times when we must wait. But in God's timing it will be answered.

Once we can recognize the answer to prayer, we will understand how much God is working in our life. Prayer gives us a keen appreciation that God will answer the prayer. So now, we ought to be careful what we pray for because we have a full expectation that it will be answered, and God will enjoy blessing us in His special way. We live in anticipation of the answer to our prayer. It is going to happen.

The Bible provides clear guidance on when we should pray. We should *"give ourselves continually to prayer"* (Acts 6:4 NKJV), "continuing *steadfastly* in prayer" (Rom 12:12 NKJV), *"praying always with all prayer and supplication in the Spirit"* (Eph 6:18 NKJV), and "pray *without ceasing"* (1 Thes 5:17 NKJV). Praying to God should be a continual conversation from the time we wake up until the time we go to sleep.

There is a time and place for dedicated prayer, like a war room (for prayer). This is a special time and place that we get alone with God. Jesus describes such a time, *"But you, when you pray, go into your room, and when you have shut your door, pray to your Father who is in the secret place; and your Father who sees in secret will reward you openly."* (Matthew 6:6 NKJV) Jesus' point here is to not make a show out of praying because then it is all about us. It needs to be all about God.

God wants us to pray, *"Ask, and it will be given to you; seek, and you will find; knock, and it will be opened to you."* (Matthew 7:7 NKJV)

Adoration, Confession, Thanksgiving, and Supplication (ACTS) is used to teach folks to pray. Too often we go straight to Supplication;

that is asking for something. Adoration is praising God for who He is and what He has done for us. Confession is realizing that we are a sinner and acknowledging that before God. Thanksgiving is a grateful acknowledgement of all the God has done for us. And then comes supplication. Requesting God's mercy, blessing, and grace in and on our life. This acronym follows the Lord's prayer where Jesus teaches His disciples to pray, *"So He said to them, 'When you pray, say: Our Father in heaven, hallowed be Your name. Your kingdom come. Your will be done on earth as it is in heaven. Give us day by day our daily bread. And forgive us our trespasses, as we forgive those that have trespassed against us. And lead us not into temptation but deliver us from the evil. For yours is the Kingdom, the Power and the Glory.'"* (Luke 11:2–4, Matt 6:9–13 NKJV)

Christianity is hard because our sin can separate us from God temporarily. We are still eternally saved if we have accepted Christ in heart. We are still a child of God. But we can be temporarily separated from God because of unconfessed sin in our lives, *"But your iniquities have separated you from your God; And your sins have hidden His face from you, so that He will not hear."* (Isaiah 59:2 NKJV) And in that time of unconfessed sin, God does not hear our prayers, *"If I regard iniquity in my heart, The Lord will not hear."* (Psalm 66:18 NKJV) We must first humble ourselves and ask the Holy Spirit to reveal all those areas of our life that we have not turned over to God. Confess our sin today and acknowledge Jesus as Lord. We will need to be in total submission to God. We need to confess our sins and return to a right relationship with Christ if we truly expect Him to work in our lives, *"If we confess our sins, He is faithful and just to forgive us our sins and to cleanse us from all unrighteousness."* (1 John 1:9 NKJV)

Repetitive prayers have always seemed unnecessary. God heard us the first time. The Bible mentions repetitive prayers, *"And when you pray, do not use vain repetitions as the heathen do. For they think that they will be heard for their many words."* (Matthew 6:7 NKJV) That doesn't mean that we don't repeat prayers—we do. God has already heard our prayer and is working it. God already knows what we will pray before we pray it, *"Therefore do not be like them. For your Father knows the things you have need of before you ask Him.*" (Matt 6:8 NKJV) So then, why even pray? Prayer is the acknowledgment of our need of God. It is a demonstration of our faith. Praying the prayer once is necessary. Praying it multiple times provides us comfort and relief. Praying a prayer over again alleviates the stress we are feeling about the situation. It takes us out of the equation and gives it back to God.

When we repeat prayers, it is for us. It reminds us that God has it. Repeated prayers keep us grounded in the fact that we have already turned it over to God and that we need to trust Him and not fix it ourselves.

There is an example in the Bible of repetitive prayer being effective. It is more a parable of persistence, "*And shall God not avenge His own elect who cry out day and night to Him, though He bears long with them? I tell you that He will avenge them speedily.*" And then the Lord asks this question, "*Nevertheless, when the Son of Man comes, will He really find faith on the earth?*" (Luke 18:7–8 NKJV) Prayers are more about faith than they are persistence.

Praying with faith is key, "*But let him ask in faith, with no doubting, for he who doubts is like a wave of the sea driven and tossed by the wind. For let not that man suppose that he will receive anything from the Lord.*" (James 1:6–7 NKJV) We must believe it will come true, "*Therefore I say to you, whatever things you ask when you pray, believe that you receive them, and you will have them.*" (Mark 11:24 NKJV)

Christianity is hard because the effects of unbelief are real. Those effects are that God doesn't work or "do many mighty works" in our life. Jesus went back to where He grew up. The people from his home area did not believe in Him. So Jesus says, "*A prophet is not without honor except in his own country and in his own house.*" Now He did not do many mighty works there because of their unbelief." (Matthew 13:57–58 NKJV)

And again, in Hebrews, we see the effects of unbelief, "*And to whom did He swear that they would not enter His rest, but to those who did not obey? So we see that they could not enter in because of unbelief.*" (Hebrews 3:18–19 NKJV) This rest is the same type of rest as when God rested on the seventh day. We want to be able to enter that rest. This rest is like what we had when we were in the Garden of Eden before we were cursed with work, "*Cursed is the ground for your sake; In toil you shall eat of it All the days of your life.*" (Genesis 3:17b NKJV) We also want to make sure everyone else enters this rest, "*Let us therefore be diligent to enter that rest, lest anyone fall according to the same example of disobedience.*" (Hebrews 4:11 NKJV) The effects of unbelief are that we will not enter the rest of the Lord.

Christianity is hard because some things take prayer and fasting, "*And when they had come to the multitude, a man came to Him, kneeling down to Him and saying, 'Lord, have mercy on my son, for he is an epileptic and suffers severely; for he often falls into the fire and often into the water. So I brought him to Your disciples, but they could not cure him.' Then Jesus answered and said, 'O faithless and perverse generation, how long shall I be with you? How long shall I bear with you? Bring him here to Me.' And Jesus rebuked the demon, and it came out of him; and the child was cured from that very hour. Then the disciples came to Jesus privately and said, 'Why could we not cast it out?' So Jesus said to them, 'Because of your unbelief; for assuredly, I say to you, if you have faith as a mustard seed, you will say to this mountain, "Move from here to there," and it will move; and nothing will be impossible for you. However, this kind does not go out except by prayer and fasting.'*" (Matthew 17:14–21 NKJV)

Crying out to the Lord is a form of prayer. It is usually a prayer of desperation. It is during a time of great need, "*And when the disciples saw Him walking on the sea, they were troubled, saying, 'It is a ghost!' And they cried out for fear.*" (Matt 14:26 NKJV)

"*And behold, two blind men sitting by the road, when they heard that Jesus was passing by, cried out, saying, 'Have mercy on us, O Lord, Son of David!'*" (Matt 22:30 NKJV)

Any answered prayer is a gift of God. We should be humbled that He would even entertain our petitions, let alone answer them. He is God. And yet His Son says, "*Most assuredly, I say to you, whatever you ask the Father in My name He will give you.*" (John 16:23a NKJV) Jesus paid the price so that we can ask the Father for His blessing on our life.

We pray to a God who loves us and wants the best for us. The issue here is who determines what is best for any given person. God determines what is best for us, not us. Most folks think that they know what the best is, at least for themselves. This becomes a main point in answering prayers. People are frustrated when their prayers aren't answered how they think they should be answered. God answers prayers according to His will, "*Now this is the confidence that we have in Him, that if we ask anything according to His will, He hears us.*" (1 John 5:14 NKJV) God knows what is best for us. Do you believe it?

Christianity is hard because God doesn't owe us anything. He already gave us life, a place to live (earth), and instructions on how to live. If we love Him, then we should follow His instructions, "*If you love Me, keep My commandments.*" (John 14:15 NKJV) If we don't follow His instructions, He can only marvel at why man makes such decisions (read the chapter on Choice) as to not follow His instructions, "*Then Jesus answered and said, 'O faithless and perverse generation, how long shall I be with you and bear with you? Bring your son here.'*" (Luke 9:41 NKJV)

Christianity is hard because God will have compassion on whom He will have compassion, "*Then God said, 'I will be gracious to whom I will be gracious, and I will have compassion on whom I will have compassion.'*" (Exodus 33:19 NKJV) We should pray that God will have compassion and be gracious toward us. God answers prayer to His glory. If the answer to prayer is no or wait, it doesn't mean that:

1. God doesn't love us
2. God is punishing us
3. God doesn't care
4. God doesn't know us
5. It doesn't mean that we don't have faith or prayed with enough faith.

God is going to do what God is going to do. Maybe God has something better for us. It is important to stay true to God during this time of trial. We don't know the ways of God. We don't know what He has in store for us. Turning our back or away from God isn't the answer. That is exactly what Satan wants us to do. God wants the best for us. We need to rest in that truth. Do you believe it?

Christianity is hard because sometimes God is making us wait or says no to our prayers. It doesn't mean that He isn't real or doesn't care. When He doesn't make our plans work to our timeline or desired end state, it doesn't mean that He doesn't care or love us. To be content when He doesn't meet our perceived plan for our life is hard to do. It takes trust. Our flesh battles on with our mind. Our perception of what our life should be or could be does not align with God's plan for our life. Will we have the ability to accept God's plan for our life? How will we know? Abraham asks this question (Gen 15:8 NKJV). So does Zachariah (Luke 1:18 NKJV). Do we really believe that God cares about little us enough to have a plan for our life and hold us to it? That is hard to grasp. Only through many trials and tribulations can we come to realize that trusting God is the only answer.

Christianity is hard because we can never know God's full purpose for our lives. Here are some examples from the Bible of key people of faith who had to wonder what God was doing in their life. If God didn't lock up Paul in a Roman prison, he would have been too busy to write most of the New Testament. If God didn't have Joseph's brother try to kill him, then he wouldn't have ever been in the position to become part of the Egyptian leadership. God wants to use us. The heroes of faith (Hebrews chapter 11) would treat God the same regardless of their circumstances. God deserves it. He will deliver us. Do we believe it? He may have to put us in an impossible situation first, ugh! He is saying to us, *Trust Me "for I will surely deliver you, and you shall not fall by the sword; but your life shall be as a prize to you, because you have put your trust in Me,' says the LORD."* (Jeremiah 39:18 NKJV)

"My soul longs, yes, even faints For the courts of the LORD; My heart and my flesh cry out for the living God." (Psalm 84:2 NKJV) Please know that when we are in trouble, crying out to the Lord is our normal response.

We pray hard for the Lord to solve our problem or take away what ails us. We ought to praise Him in these times.

Praise acknowledges our Lord and Savior. It gives Him the acknowledgement that we will still praise Him in our lowest points. After being beaten for sharing the gospel, Paul and Silas are singing hymns (praises) to God. They were staying true to God, "*And when they had laid many stripes on them, they threw them into prison, commanding the jailer to keep them securely. Having received such a charge, he put them into the inner prison and fastened their feet in the stocks. But at midnight Paul and Silas were praying and singing hymns to God, and the prisoners were listening to them. Suddenly there was a great earthquake, so that the foundations of the prison were shaken; and immediately all the doors were opened, and everyone's chains were loosed.*" (Acts 16:23–26 NKJV) Paul and Silas stayed true to God regardless of their situation. God put them in that situation to bring glory to His name by providing for them in an impossible situation.

It is heartening to see that we are not the only one to make rash promises when under stress and crying out to the Lord for help. Here the psalmist cries out and makes promises we have proven we can't keep. That promise is to keep the law. It is good to the have the intent, but it is only through the strength and love of Jesus Christ can we even entertain keeping God's statutes and word. It is good to seek the Lord with all our heart, soul, and mind as the psalmist does here.

"*I cry out with my whole heart; Hear me, O Lord! I will keep Your statutes. I cry out to You; Save me, and I will keep Your testimonies. I rise before the dawning of the morning, and cry for help; I hope in Your word. My eyes are awake through the night watches, That I may meditate on Your word. Hear my voice according to Your lovingkindness; O LORD, revive me according to Your justice.*" (Psalm 119:145–149 NKJV)

Be careful not to make promises in a prayer that we cannot keep, "*When you make a vow to God, do not delay to pay it; For He has no pleasure in fools. Pay what you have vowed—Better not to vow than to vow and not pay.*" (Ecclesiastes 5:4–5 NKJV)

Personal application – I have had the privilege of having a prayer warrior pray for me and teach me to pray. I met with an Army Sergeant Major on a weekly basis. He was a prayer warrior. That is a person who will pray for everyone and anyone at a moment's notice. Prayer warriors are very intentional about praying. Every time I hear this verse, this man of God comes to my mind, "*The effective, fervent prayer of a righteous man avails much.*" (James 5:16b NKJV) His prayer life affected me that much. He prayed with real faith and full anticipation that it would come true. It is either funny or ironic or just sad that I can remember all of these and have trouble remembering his name. He left a legacy of prayer with me. He taught me what prayer was all about. I will forever be thankful.

Prayer is talking to God. Like any other relationship, it takes work. Figuring out how to trust God in all situations, even and especially when it doesn't go how we think, is what this faith journey is all about. Having a solid prayer life will allow us to converse with Almighty and Holy God. Remembering who God is and what He wants will help make our prayer life more effective.

Pray that we all live in anticipation of God's answer to our prayers.

CHAPTER 12

TEST OUR FAITH, GOD WILL

"That the genuineness of your faith, being much more precious than gold that perishes, though it is tested by fire, may be found to praise, honor, and glory at the revelation of Jesus Christ."

(1 PETER 1:7 NKJV)

C hristianity is hard because it constantly requires us to use our faith, which is tested by every choice we make. Faith is defined in Hebrews, *"Now faith is the substance of things hoped for, the evidence of things not seen."* (Heb 11:1 NKJV) Faith is believing that God exists without the evidence. No one really knows for sure. That is why it is faith. If we knew for sure, then it wouldn't be faith.

Jesus invites us to believe in Him. Faith is the act of believing. Jesus' ministry was for us to believe in Him, *"Jesus answered and said to them, 'This is the work of God, that you believe in Him whom He sent'"* (Jn 6:29 NKJV) and God wrote the Bible so that we may believe and have life. *"And truly Jesus did many other signs in the presence of His disciples, which are not written in this book; but these are written that you may believe that Jesus is the Christ, the Son of God, and that believing you may have life in His name."* (John 20:30–31 NKJV) Do we believe it?

Unless we test our faith, how do we know it is real? In 2 Corinthians,

Paul writes to test ourselves to see if we indeed believe. Examine our life and whether we live for Christ or are we still obstinate, *"Examine yourselves as to whether you are in the faith. Test yourselves. Do you not know yourselves, that Jesus Christ is in you?—unless indeed you are disqualified."* (2 Cor 13:5 NKJV)

Testing of our faith requires for us to step out on our faith. This usually starts a battle in our mind and heart. These questions and statements come to our mind when we try to use our faith: Is this really from God? This makes no sense. Can God really care about me? Why would the God of the universe be involved with me? Surely, He has more important things to do than test me or ask me to test myself. These are all questions that Satan puts in our heads. We need to get out of our head and follow the Spirit's guidance.

It is important for us to test our own faith. It helps us continue to believe and grow our faith. All the questions above are designed to keep us from walking out our faith. Those questions are what makes it so difficult to believe. When we think about it too long, we can talk ourselves out of using our faith, *"Trust in the LORD with all your heart, and lean not on your own understanding; In all your ways acknowledge Him, And He shall direct your paths."* (Proverbs 3:5–6 NKJV) Faith takes trust. We can't work it out in our head first. It is a matter of the heart. There is no final solution or ability to game the system. The only action left is to trust God and step out on faith.

We are to accept Christ with a childlike faith. A simple faith of total trust. *"Assuredly, I say to you, whoever does not receive the kingdom of God as a little child will by no means enter it."* (Luke 18:17 NKJV) We start to drift and waver in our faith if we think about it too long. A child doesn't think about it. The point isn't to stop growing in our faith or mature in our walk, but to remember and apply our faith as a child would. God the Father is worthy of that level of trust. Do we believe it? Like a child?

Christianity is hard because it requires constant nurturing. Staying in the Word of God is a key here as well, *"So then faith comes by hearing, and hearing by the word of God."* (Rom 10:17 NKJV) Reading the Bible daily strengthens our faith. It is one of the tools to use when Satan comes at us with all the doubts and attacks. Anything that we want to do from faith should be consistent with the Word of God. If we think we are doing something counter to the Bible, then read and pray about it. Seek God with all our heart, mind, and soul and He will direct our paths.

God will test our hearts and our faith, "*The refining pot is for silver and the furnace for gold, But the LORD tests the hearts.*" (Proverbs 17:3 NKJV) God already knows how we are going to respond. So the testing is for us. He wants us to prove to ourselves that we believe and to understand His power in us.

Christianity is hard because we must stay true to God. God can use anyone and anytime to do His will. God will often test a person first to see if he will make wise choices. Whether he will see God's will through to completion. Here is where Paul is writing about God using Him, "*But as we have been approved by God to be entrusted with the gospel, even so we speak, not as pleasing men, but God who tests our hearts.*" (1 Thessalonians 2:4 NKJV) God tests the hearts to see what manner of person we are, "*And you shall remember that the LORD your God led you all the way these forty years in the wilderness, to humble you and test you, to know what was in your heart, whether you would keep His commandments or not.*" (Deuteronomy 8:2 NKJV) God tests us to see if we are willing to be obedient and humble. That is the type of person He can use.

Now, some of us will say that is a mean God. Doesn't He love us? Yes, He loves us and always will. But to be used by Him is a different story. We can't have it both ways. On one hand be defiant, proud, and self-serving and on the other want to be used of God. It doesn't work that way, "*For where envy and self-seeking exist, confusion and every evil thing are there. But the wisdom that is from above is first pure, then peaceable, gentle, willing to yield, full of mercy and good fruits, without partiality and without hypocrisy.*" (James 3:16–17 NKJV) He may still use us but not how we think or in a way that we like.

For example, God raises up people to fulfill His will even when they don't realize He is using them. Here God raises up a prophet to provide guidance to the nation of Israel, "*The LORD your God will raise up for you a Prophet like me from your midst, from your brethren. Him you shall hear.*" (Deuteronomy 18:15 NKJV) And again, here He raises up a priest, "*Then I will raise up for Myself a faithful priest who shall do according to what is in My heart and in My mind. I will build him a sure house, and he shall walk before My anointed forever.*" (1 Samuel 2:35 NKJV) God will even raise up a whole nation to fulfill His will and purpose, "*But, behold, I will raise up a nation against you, O house of Israel.*" (Amos 6:14a NKJV)

Christianity is hard because Satan will also test our faith. He will attack us, "*Be sober, be vigilant; because your adversary the devil walks about like a roaring lion, seeking whom he may devour.*" (1 Peter 5:8 NKJV) Many people fall at this point. They give into Satan's ploys. Satan tries to keep us from serving God. He has no power over us except what we let him have, "*Therefore submit to God. Resist the devil and he will flee from you.*" (James 4:7 NKJV) By choosing the Lord, Satan loses his power over us, but he will try, nonetheless. He can be very convincing. And he knows all our weaknesses and will test every one of them repeatedly.

God will also test us to see if we are going to obedient, "*And Moses said to the people, 'Do not fear; for God has come to test you, and that His fear may be before you, so that you may not sin.'*" (Exodus 20:20 NKJV) When we are in awe of the love and grace bestowed on us by God, it will provide power to us to resist sin.

God tests our hearts, and really our faith, to prepare us to serve Him. Some examples from the Bible are Paul on the Damascus road (Acts 9:1–20 NKJV), Abraham with Isaac, "*By faith Abraham, when he was tested, offered up Isaac, and he who had received the promises offered up his only begotten son*" (Hebrews 11:17 NKJV), and David waiting to take the Kingdom.

God works in the lives of people of faith. Jesus frequently asked this question (do you believe that I am able to do this?) of the people looking to be healed, "*And when He had come into the house, the blind men came to Him. And Jesus said to them, 'Do you believe that I am able to do this?'*

They said to Him, 'Yes, Lord.' Then He touched their eyes, saying, 'According to your faith let it be to you.'" (Matt 9:28–29 NKJV)

Do we believe it? This is the test. Do we ever feel that Jesus is asking us, "Do you believe that I am able to do this?" What is our answer? It has nothing to do with us or our feelings of inadequacy. It is a matter of Jesus' capability and willingness to assist us. Get ourselves out of the way, just believe. Our belief in Him and His works unleashes His willingness to work in our lives, *"Now He did not do many mighty works there because of their unbelief."* (Matt 13:58 NKJV)

Christianity is hard because sometimes we fail the test. God will test our faith. What happens when we don't pass the test—which is the case too often? We were raised to be independent and take charge. To give up that independence and control without knowing the result goes against everything we grew up believing or were taught. But when we fail to follow God's direction for our life, God is gracious. He will work with us where we are in our faith journey. He loves us and His desire is for us to come to be complete in Jesus Christ, *"till we all come to the unity of the faith and of the knowledge of the Son of God, to a perfect man, to the measure of the stature of the fullness of Christ."* (Ephesians 4:13 NKJV)

Jesus provides a story about a father who prays to Jesus about helping him with his unbelief. After asking Jesus' disciples to heal his son stricken with an evil spirit, the father engages Jesus in a conversation about the son. As part of the conversation, *"Jesus said to him, 'If you can believe, all things are possible to him who believes.'"* In response to this statement, *"Immediately the father of the child cried out and said with tears, 'Lord, I believe; help my unbelief!'"* (Mark 9:23–24 NKJV) God is able. Do we believe it? God, help us all with our unbelief.

Christianity is hard because we must continue to believe. Just as the law required obedience, faith requires belief. For faith to work, one must continue to believe. Wavering in our faith can cause us to stumble, *"But let him ask in faith, with no doubting, for he who doubts is like a wave of the sea driven and tossed by the wind. For let not that man suppose that he will receive anything from the Lord; he is a double-minded man, unstable in all his ways.*" (James 1:6–8 NKJV) Faith takes total trust in God to accomplish His purpose in our life. Even if we don't understand it. It is a childlike faith. Trust that the Father will take care of us.

Under the law, we sinned if we didn't follow the rules. We didn't obey. That is called sin. Faith requires us to act on our beliefs. If we don't walk by faith, it is a sin, "*for whatever is not from faith is sin.*" (Rom 14:23b NKJV) To not act out of faith is a sin. That should change how we look at faith. Unbelief in Jesus is a sin. Jesus says, "*But whoever denies Me before men, him I will also deny before My Father who is in heaven.*" (Matthew 10:33 NKJV)

Christianity is hard because the answer to our prayers is sometimes wait, maybe, or no. Our faith is really tested when we perceive that God hasn't answer our prayer. We really begin to question our faith, "*So, Jesus answered and said to them, 'Have faith in God. For assuredly, I say to you, whoever says to this mountain, "Be removed and be cast into the sea," and does not doubt in his heart, but believes that those things he says will be done, he will have whatever he says. Therefore, I say to you, whatever things you ask when you pray, believe that you receive them, and you will have them.*'" (Mark 11:22–24 NKJV) When God doesn't answer a prayer in our timing or way, many thoughts go through our heads. Is it because we don't have enough faith? Is it not God's will? Is it because we are not worthy? Why is God not answering our prayer? Have we done something wrong? Do we need to confess it?

Which one of these questions is it? What can we do or not do to fix this situation and get past it? Our nature is to correct the problem and move on. Maybe God wants us to just wait. Is it because He has something better for us? We are not very good at waiting. For us to wait on the Lord and not do anything is very difficult for many of us to do. And how do we know that is the problem? Who says there is a problem? Maybe the problem is we must wait. Can we be content in the Lord? Patiently wait and be happy about it? Is this a test? How do we know?

And what does the testing of our faith produce? Patience. And patience leads to being perfect and complete. And James tells us that we should count it all as joy, "*My brethren, count it all joy when you fall into* various trials, knowing that the testing of your faith produces patience. But let patience have its perfect work, that you may be perfect and complete, lacking nothing." (James 1:2–4 NKJV) When Jesus is enough, we can count it all as joy.

All our works are going to be tested. Our works will be tested by fire, "For no other foundation can anyone lay than that which is laid, which is Jesus Christ. Now if anyone builds on this foundation with gold, silver, precious stones, wood, hay, straw, each one's work will become clear; for the Day will declare it, because it will be revealed by fire; and the fire will test each one's work, of what sort it is. If anyone's work which he has built on it endures, he will receive a reward. If anyone's work is burned, he will suffer loss; but he himself will be saved, yet so as through fire." (1 Corinthians 3:11–15 NKJV) Our salvation is secure. We will make it through the fire. It is the fruits of our faith that will be tested by fire to determine whether it is of the Lord. This is again a heart issue. Are we doing everything for the Lord?

Besides testing ourselves and having God test us, He instructs us to test the Spirits, "Beloved, do not believe every spirit, but test the spirits, whether they are of God; because many false prophets have gone out into the world. By this you know the Spirit of God: Every spirit that confesses that Jesus Christ has come in the flesh is of God." (1 John 4:1–2 NKJV) Before we believe someone else, we should check to see if it is consistent with the word of God. In fact, we are instructed to "test all things; hold fast what is good. Abstain from every form of evil." (1 Thessalonians 5:21–22 NKJV) By testing our own faith and testing the spirits, we can discern between good and evil; therefore, making good choices to stay away from evil.

Christianity is hard because testing reveals what is in your heart. It is the point of the testing, "I know also, my God, that You test the heart and have pleasure in uprightness. As for me, in the uprightness of my heart I have willingly offered all these things; and now with joy I have seen Your people, who are present here to offer willingly to You." (1 Chronicles 29:17 NKJV) If we are being obedient for the wrong reasons, it won't produce fruit. One of the main reasons is pride, "Take heed that you do not do your *charitable deeds before men, to be seen by them. Otherwise you have no reward from your Father in heaven.*" (Matthew 6:1 NKJV) This is a test is to see if we will present ourselves willingly and humbly to God. Our works should be out of love and willingness to serve and not out of coercion or for a reward.

Testing is another way God relates to us. God tests us to bring us to a point of understanding of our need of Him. He wants us to be His people, "*I will bring the one-third through the fire, will refine them as silver is refined, And test them as gold is tested. They will call on My name, And I will answer them. I will say, 'This is My people'; And each one will say, 'The LORD is my God.*" (Zech 13:9 NKJV) It is only through Christ that we can accomplish anything. God wants to be our God and for us to be His people.

Test our faith. Try it out. Trust the Lord today. The prayer for all of us is "*that the genuineness of your faith, being much more precious than gold that perishes, though it is tested by fire, may be found to praise, honor, and glory at the revelation of Jesus Christ.*" (1 Peter 1:7 NKJV)

CHAPTER 13

WALK BY FAITH

"For we walk by faith, not by sight."

(2 CORINTHIANS 5:7 NKJV)

Christianity is hard because God wants us to walk before Him and be blameless. We are anything but blameless. Our sin nature persists. That is why He sent His only Son to restore us to being blameless in His sight because of what Jesus has done, *"When Abram was ninety-nine years old, the LORD appeared to Abram and said to him, "I am Almighty God; walk before Me and be blameless."* (Genesis 17:1 NKJV)

The Bible uses the word "walk" to describe how to live life. And often it refers to living life in obedience. Here God is instructing Moses about the manna. He wants to see whether they will obey or not. *"Then the LORD said to Moses, 'Behold, I will rain bread from heaven for you. And the people shall go out and gather a certain quota every day, that I my test them, whether they will walk in My law or not.'"* (Exodus 16:4 NKJV)

God once walked with us in the Garden of Eden, *"And they heard the sound of the LORD God walking in the garden in the cool of the day, and Adam and his wife hid themselves from the presence of the LORD God among the trees of the garden. Then the LORD God called to Adam and said to him, "Where are you?"* (Genesis 3:8–9 NKJV) God loves us, but sin has separated us from God. God wants to walk with us again as He once walked with us in the Garden of Eden, *"As God has said: 'I will dwell in them And walk among them. I will be their God, And they shall be My people'"* (2 Corinthians 6:16b NKJV) Many people expect the Christian experience to be like the Garden of Eden experience. They fall away from the faith when they find out that Christianity isn't like the Garden of Eden yet.

Jesus restored the relationship and provided a way for us to walk, *"There is therefore now no condemnation to those who are in Christ Jesus, who do not walk according to the flesh, but according to the Spirit."* (Romans 8:1 NKJV) No condemnation for those who walk by the Spirit.

The story of the Pharisee and the tax collector is a story of being humble. (Luke 18:9–14 NKJV) Even if we are trying to do the right things, like the Pharisee thought he was doing, we are still sinners and need to humble ourselves before a holy God, *"God, be merciful to me a sinner!"* (Luke 18:13 NKJV) Doing things won't get us into heaven. Only having faith that Jesus exists, died for our sins, rose from the dead to restore our relationship to God, and accept Him as our Lord and Savior will let us enter the grace of God. No matter how right we think we are with God, we need to stay humble and understand that it is only by His grace that we can do anything.

In King David's instruction at his deathbed to his son Solomon, he states to walk properly before God, *"And keep the charge of the LORD your God: to walk in His ways, to keep His statutes, His commandments, His judgments, and His testimonies, as it is written in the Law of Moses, that you may prosper in all that you do and wherever you turn; that the LORD may fulfill His word which He spoke concerning me, saying, 'If your sons take heed to their way, to walk before Me in truth with all their heart and with all their soul,' He said, 'you shall not lack a man on the throne of Israel.'"* (1 Kings 2:3–4 NKJV)

Here are some examples of our walk before God:

Walk in love and obedience – *"This is love, that we walk according to His commandments. This is the commandment, that as you have heard from the beginning, you should walk in it."*

(2 JOHN 1:6 NKJV)

"For we are His workmanship, created in Christ Jesus for good works, which God prepared beforehand that we should walk in them."

(EPHESIANS 2:10 NKJV)

Walk worthy – *"I, therefore, the prisoner of the Lord, beseech you to walk worthy of the calling with which you were called, with all lowliness and gentleness, with longsuffering, bearing with one another in love, endeavoring to keep the unity of the Spirit in the bond of peace."*

(EPHESIANS 4:1–3 NKJV)

"For this reason we also, since the day we heard it, do not cease to pray for you, and to ask that you may be filled with the knowledge of His will in all wisdom and spiritual understanding; that you may walk worthy of the Lord, fully pleasing Him, being fruitful in every good work and increasing in the knowledge of God; strengthened with all might, according to His glorious power, for all patience and longsuffering with joy; giving thanks to the Father who has quali-fied us to be partakers of the inheritance of the saints in the light."

(COLOSSIANS 1:9–12 NKJV)

Walk in truth – *"For I rejoiced greatly when brethren came and testified of the truth that is in you, just as you walk in the truth. I have no greater joy than to hear that my children walk in truth."*

(3 JOHN 1:3-4 NKJV)

"Teach me Your way, O LORD; I will walk in Your truth; Unite my heart to fear Your name."

(PSALM 86:11 NKJV)

Walk in love – *"And walk in love, as Christ also has loved us and given Himself for us, an offering and a sacrifice to God for a sweet-smelling aroma."*

(EPHESIANS 5:2 NKJV)

Walk as children of light – *"For you were once darkness, but now you are light in the Lord. Walk as children of light (for the fruit of the Spirit is in all goodness, righteousness, and truth), finding out what is acceptable to the Lord."*

(EPHESIANS 5:8–10 NKJV)

Walk circumspectly – *"See then that you walk circumspectly, not as fools but as wise, redeeming the time, because the days are evil."*

(EPHESIANS 5:15–16 NKJV)

Here are two examples of how not to walk – *"How they told you that there would be mockers in the last time who would walk according to their own ungodly lusts."*

(JUDE 1:18 NKJV)

"I will bring distress upon men, And they shall walk like blind men, Because they have sinned against the LORD; Their blood shall be poured out like dust, And their flesh like refuse."

(ZEPHANIAH 1:17 NKJV)

How we walk in this life is a choice. We can choose to walk in the light or walk in the darkness, *"Then Jesus spoke to them again, saying, "I am the light of the world. He who follows Me shall not walk in darkness but have the light of life."*

(JOHN 8:12 NKJV)

Walking in the dark isn't a good thing, *"Then Jesus said to them, 'A little while longer the light is with you. Walk while you have the light, lest darkness overtake you; he who walks in darkness does not know where he is going.'"*

(JOHN 12:35 NKJV)

"This I say, therefore, and testify in the Lord, that you should no longer walk as the rest of the Gentiles walk, in the futility of their mind, having their understanding darkened, being alienated from the life of God, because of the ignorance that is in them, because of the blindness of their heart; who, being past feeling, have given themselves over to lewdness, to work all uncleanness with greediness."

(EPHESIANS 4:17–19 NKJV)

Our final walk for those who are saved will be in heaven in the light of God's glory. *"And the nations of those who are saved shall walk in its light, and the kings of the earth bring their glory and honor into it."* (Revelation 21:24 NKJV) That will be a sweet walk. We ought to get goose bumps even thinking about it. Our world will be back to how people think it ought to be now. We had it that way once in the Garden of Eden. And when we walk in the new Jerusalem, we will be fully restored in our relationship to God. Thank you, Jesus!

Christianity is hard because we still have a sin nature. As evidence by the history of Israel, there is a cycle that humans go through in relation to God, our spiritual biorhythm.

There is a spiritual biorhythm that Christians experience walking out their faith. The highs and joy of obedience. The lows and discipline of disobedience. Is there a way to level the peaks and valleys to have a more consistent walk with God? This requires a conscience choice to smooth out the ups and downs. We would be close to God, feeling the peace and joy that is so clearly described in the Bible. Then we would start to fall away. We learned that when we are at the top of the Christian experience is when we need to stay closer to God. Most Christians feel closest, seek or cry out to God when they are in the midst of the valley, when they are sinning or in a tribulation. If we could only learn to act in such a way when we are at the top, then we could level the peaks and valleys to have a more consistent walk with God.

The Old Testament is full of stories where the nation of Israel would find themselves in such a cycle. Israel would fall away from God and find themselves in the valley. They would experience the consequences of sin and they would start to seek God again. They would seek God until they were on the peak again where they would then leave God out of their decisions. Then the whole cycle would start over.

Moses is giving instructions from the Lord to Israel, "*Beware that you do not forget the LORD your God by not keeping His commandments, His judgments, and His statutes which I command you today.*" (Deuteronomy 8:11 NKJV) Moses proceeds to talk about the blessings that Israel will receive from the Lord. He explains that when they are full and life is good, they will forget about the Lord, "*Then it shall be, if you by any means forget the LORD your God, and follow other gods, and serve them and worship them, I testify against you this day that you shall surely perish.*" (Deuteronomy 8:19 NKJV) And the cycle repeats itself. The key is found in verse 18, "*And you shall remember the LORD your God, for it is He who gives you power to get wealth.*" (Deuteronomy 8:18a NKJV) The key is to remember where and how we received the blessings whether life is good or bad.

The only way to level the biorhythm out is to seek God with the fervor while we are on the mountain that we seek Him when we are in tribulation, "*And He said to me, 'My grace is sufficient for you, for My strength is made perfect in weakness.'*" (2 Cor 12:9 NKJV)

Devotional – Cycle of Sin and Forgiveness

After I sin, I go through the same mental exercise over and over again. The process goes like this: I feel regret. I feel guilty. I ask for forgiveness. I realize I am free in Christ. But there remains a consequence of sin. I pray for forgiveness and mercy understanding that the grace of Jesus Christ has covered me and paid all my sins. I specifically pray for mercy so that God withholds the consequences of sin from me. I get mad at myself for being weak and not trusting in Christ and believing that He is strong enough for me. I wonder how Christ could ever love me and continue to love me. Why would he do that when I continue to fail him? When I continue to fall victim to sin, to give into temptations? I feel unworthy as a Christian and a follower of Christ. If it keeps me from serving Christ, then who gets the victory? Who gets the glory?

Then I evolve to this thought process. I really do love the Lord. And it hurts me when I sin. I feel I have damaged the relationship. I again get mad at myself for not being faithful member of the relationship. I want to quickly restore the relationship.

I have been through this cycle since I became a Christian, although it is less frequent now. I pray and hope that at some point, I will break the cycle. I have had some success from time to time. But never real victory over sin. The key is to rely on Christ in me. Rely on His strength and power. I cannot beat this cycle on my own. The only way to beat this cycle is to have Christ work through me. This makes being a Christian very hard for me. Even after believing and knowing this to be true, the cycle still happens. Is the flesh really that strong?

Paul wrote about this struggle, "*For what I am doing, I do not understand. For what I will to do, that I do not practice; but what I hate, that I do. If, then, I do what I will not to do, I agree with the law that it is good. But now, it is no longer I who do it, but sin that dwells in me. For I know that in me (that is, in my flesh) nothing good dwells; for to will is present with me, but how to perform what is good I do not find. For the good that I will to do, I do not do; but the evil I will not to do, that I practice. Now if I do what I will not to do, it is no longer I who do it, but sin that dwells in me.*" (Romans 7:15–20 NKJV)

So why do I fail so often? Is it that I underestimate the power of sin and the desires of my flesh? Even after knowing the destruction that sin provides, I still sin. I have been down this road so many times that I know where it leads. The end result is not something I want or desire. How can

I convince myself in the moment of temptation that the consequences of the sin act are devastating and destructive? Because I know this to be true. My sin cycle has told me time and time again that it is true. So why do I keep on sinning? But in the moment my flesh takes over and before I know it, I have sinned again. And the cycle starts over. I try praying. I try stepping away from the situation. I ask Jesus to remove it.

There are some people who claim victory over sin. They are either in denial or God hasn't revealed the sin in their life to them yet. Either way, the Bible says "*If we say that we have no sin, we deceive ourselves, and the truth is not in us*" 1 John 1:8 (NKJV).

The best thing for me is to avoid placing myself in the situation to be tempted, "*But each one is tempted when he is drawn away by his own desires and enticed. Then, when desire has conceived, it gives birth to sin; and sin, when it is full-grown, brings forth death.*" (James 1:14–15 NKJV) Reflecting on God's truth. Reciting the Bible. Telling myself the truth and not dwelling on the temptation. Trying to mentally beat the temptation has limited success at best. This is why it is so important to read the Bible every day to keep God's word fresh in our mind. We must use God's word. By the way, this is how Christ fought off Satan. He used the word of God. Christ provided the example to us. Paul concludes that we are more than conquerors through Jesus Christ, "*Yet in all these things we are more than conquerors through Him who loved us.*" (Romans 8:37 NKJV) Make the choice to live life through Jesus Christ.

We are to walk in the Spirit and not the flesh, "*There is therefore now no condemnation to those who are in Christ Jesus, who do not walk according to the flesh, but according to the Spirit.*" (Romans 8:1 NKJV) This is a daily choice if not hourly.

God loves us so much that He gives us the choice. Pray that our walk, by faith, honors God in all our actions today, "*Therefore, whether you eat or drink, or whatever you do, do all to the glory of God.*" (1 Corinthians 10:31 NKJV)

CHAPTER 14

FAITH JOURNEY

*"Work out your own salvation with fear and trembling; for it is God
who works in you both to will and to do for His good pleasure."*
PHILIPPIANS 2:12B–13, NKJV

C hristianity is hard because we are to be Holy, *"Be holy, for I am holy."*
(1 Peter 1:16b NKJV) How is that even possible? Only by the *"grace
of the Lord Jesus Christ, and the love of God, and the communion of the
Holy Spirit."* (2 Corinthians 13:14 NKJV) There are different phases of
faith that we work through as we worked out our salvation through sanctification. Sanctification is the process of becoming holy.

God will relate to each of us at our level of spiritual maturity. Maturity
sounds wrong. Maybe it is our level of commitment to following Christ.
Maybe it is our level of believing, our level of faith. There are different
levels of believing. Matthew quotes Jesus as he describes a level of faith,
*"So Jesus said to them, 'Because of your unbelief; for assuredly, I say to you,
if you have faith as a mustard seed, you will say to this mountain, "Move
from here to there," and it will move; and nothing will be impossible for
you."'* (Matthew 17:20 NKJV) Faith as a mustard seed is a small amount
of faith because the mustard seed is the smallest of seeds.

First is the beginner level. This is the level where we have just accepted
the Lord. We are still trying to figure out what this life with the Lord is

like or how we are supposed to act. Then comes the question of what do we really believe, "*that we should no longer be children, tossed to and fro and carried about with every wind of doctrine, by the trickery of men, in the cunning craftiness of deceitful plotting.*" (Ephesians 4:14 NKJV)

During this first level, the parable of the seed is realized. (Matthew 13:3–9 NKJV) If the word of God lands on good soil, then our life and faith will produce fruit. This is possible when we have strong disciples helping us in our walk. They are feeding us with encouragement, understanding, and love. If the Word of God lands among the thorns, then the cares of the world become or stay more important to us and our faith is overcome by the cares of the world and has no room to mature. If the word of God lands on concrete, then there isn't anyone around to feed us and the faith withers from lack of encouragement, understanding, and love. If the word of God falls where the birds can eat it, then faith never really has a chance and the Word is rejected out of hand.

Personal application – This phase of the journey was much longer for me than I think is normal. I went through my desert period, or at least that is what I call it. I was determined that I could have a relationship with Christ and not with His people, especially those who went to Church. This was a long part of the journey but necessary. After accepting the Lord during a youth trip, I had a couple of months with that church before we moved. That move was hard on me and I went to the desert. I fell away. There is a lot to be learned in the desert. This is where I learned about the unending chasing after me by the Lord. He was always looking out for me. His love found me repeatedly, "*for the Son of Man has come to seek and to save that which was lost.*" (Luke 19:10 NKJV) I was lost and wandering around in the desert. Jesus found me there and met me where I was spiritually.

Depending on whether we are being fed or not will greatly impact our ability to grow in our faith. We can still grow without it, but it will be tougher. Paul sent Timothy to the church of Thessalonica to encourage and train them, *"sent Timothy, our brother and minister of God, and our fellow laborer in the gospel of Christ, to establish you and encourage you concerning your faith."* (1 Thessalonians 3:2 NKJV)

Personal application – Some great people were influential in my walk. They were a big encouragement at a time when I needed it. There was a Command Sergeant Major who would meet with me once a week and we co-led a midweek Bible study. He embodied James 5:16b NKJV, *"The effective, fervent prayer of a righteous man avails much."* And then there were my sisters in the Lord. We met for over two years studying the book of Hebrews. There were other folks who would attend the study, but it was us three for the duration. They sought God with all their heart, and it was contagious, *"Blessed are the pure in heart, For they shall see God."* (Matthew 5:8 NKJV)

Reading the Bible is important to your spiritual health, *"as newborn babes, desire the pure milk of the word, that you may grow thereby."* (1 Peter 2:2 NKJV)

Personal application – I learned this lesson from a first sergeant in the Army who was very physically fit. He related the concept of bodily exercise to spiritual exercise. You will become flabby if you don't work out. The same is true for your spiritual wellbeing, *"For bodily exercise profits a little, but godliness is profitable for all things, having promise of the life that now is and of that which is to come."* (1 Timothy 4:8 NKJV) Spiritual exercise comes with a promise of the life that is to come. Reading the Bible everyday provides you the strength, courage, and tools to fight off the temptations of the Devil. (Eph 6:11–17 NKJV)

The next level is after we have been a disciple for a while. We start to think we got this Christian thing figured out until the Lord shows us how far we must go in this faith journey. Key lessons in this phase include humility, dependency, and God's rightful place in our life.

This is the phase that we need to learn humility. We start to think that we are all that. Look at us. How spiritually mature we are. God must love us because look at all our works. That is when God will humble us. We start to realize that we can do nothing by ourselves, "*I am the vine, you are the branches. He who abides in Me, and I in him, bears much fruit; for without Me you can do nothing.*" (John 15:5 NKJV) Only through the power of Christ can we do anything. It isn't about us, so stop gloating and recognize who should receive the glory, Jesus Christ.

It is also about this time that the Lord will put a burden on us to share the Gospel, "*Go therefore and make disciples of all the nations.*" (Matthew 28:19 NKJV)

Personal application – There was a time when I wanted to save people for Christ. I felt a need to share this experience. I knew the answer and I was out to save the world. Or at least the folks the Lord would send my way. I read many books on outreach and sharing the Gospel. I was part of the outreach team at church. I went on visitation. I really had a burden for the lost—still do. I put a lot of pressure on myself to reach the lost. I didn't want to see anyone burn in Hell. I felt the pressure to say the right words or act the right way. Then after more than a few failures, I realized that it wasn't on me to save the world or anyone for that matter.

It is the Holy Spirit who convicts people to turn from their sins and accept Jesus as their Lord and Savior. Our role in sharing the Gospel is simply to tell what Jesus Christ has meant to us. We can do that. That is the Gospel. The Word of God is powerful and will do its work on people's heart. (Heb 4:12 NKJV) That takes the pressure off us. It made it much easier to share our testimony. The recipient's salvation isn't dependent on us.

We don't have to say the right thing at the right time. All the pressure is off. We can rest in the Spirit and rely on His wisdom. He will provide exactly what the other person needs to hear. It is the Spirit who saves, not us.

It is during this phase that the cares of the world can take us away, "*And I, brethren, could not speak to you as to spiritual people but as to carnal, as to babes in Christ. I fed you with milk and not with solid food; for until now you were not able to receive it, and even now you are still not able; for you are still carnal. For where there are envy, strife, and divisions among you, are you not carnal and behaving like mere men?*" (1 Corinthians 3:1–3 NKJV) Whether it is climbing the corporate ladder, fascination with celebrities, or being engrossed in sports, the lure of the world will take us away from God. Placing anything over or before God is a sin and won't satisfy in the end.

Somewhere along the path, we realize that God will be first in our life, "*But seek first the kingdom of God and His righteousness, and all these things shall be added to you.*" (Matthew 6:33 NKJV) When we get this out of order, life doesn't go well for us. God still loves us and will take care of us. God will continue to work on us to bring this back into the correct order. Once things are in the proper order, the Lord will give those items back to us to enjoy. We are to provide the first fruits of everything in our life to God as an offering (Deut 26:2 NKJV)

He starts to reveal different parts of our life that are placed higher in our life than Him. These are idols. They can be sports, music, work, and even our kids. "*If anyone comes to Me and does not hate his father and mother, wife and children, brothers and sisters, yes, and his own life also, he cannot be My disciple.*" (Luke 14:26 NKJV) This is a hard saying. Jesus wants to be first. This doesn't mean that our family isn't important or we shouldn't love them. This just highlights how important this topic is to Jesus. He will continue to work on us until it happens. It takes a while to realize that once things are in the correct order, life works better and there is joy. Jesus is enough. We cannot be dependent on our wives or kids for value. Jesus supplies all our needs. Looking to Jesus for our life is reaching a new level in our faith walk.

Christianity is hard because growing spiritually takes total reliance on the Lord. After understanding that we can do nothing of ourselves and are totally reliant on the Lord for everything, then we can begin to grow spiritually. This again is a hard phase to implement because we will be attacked by Satan, question our faith, and continue to rely on our own strength.

Now when we realize that we can't do anything good on our own, we fall to knees and commit our life again and again to the Lord. This level comes after trying to "do it" by ourselves (live the Christian life by our own strength). After years of trying and failing miserably, what we eventually learn is to lean on the Lord, trust Him, and put our life in His control. "*For though by this time you ought to be teachers, you need someone to teach you again the first principles of the oracles of God; and you have come to need milk and not solid food. For everyone who partakes only of milk is unskilled in the word of righteousness, for he is a babe. But solid food belongs to those who are of full age, that is, those who by reason of use have their senses exercised to discern both good and evil.*" (Hebrews 5:12–14 NKJV)

There comes a time when we must accept God's way and ask for our faith to be increased. To fully understand that all things are through and for Christ, "*For of Him and through Him and to Him are all things, to whom be glory forever. Amen.*" (Rom 11:36 NKJV)

There are moments along the faith journey that certain events make an impact. They force us to evaluate our faith and choose. There are events that forced us to think and defend our faith. Here is such an event:

Personal application – When our second son was born, we were looking to have him circumcised. The doctor at the time pleaded with us to not have it done. I was taken back by his insistence. Part of me can empathize with him. I still wanted to proceed with the circumcision. Maybe it was because it is part of our family history. I thought it was the right thing to do from a health issue. It would prevent infections later. The doctor quoted, "*For in Christ Jesus neither circumcision nor uncircumcision avails anything, but faith working through love.*" (Gal 5:6 NKJV) It made me really think about why I was doing it. I prayed to God about whether we should proceed or not. I wasn't doing it to gain favor with God. In the end, I decided to proceed with the circumcision as an offering to the Lord. I was giving Matthew back to God and this was my sign of that commitment. Matthew is serving the Lord today as a missionary to military kids. The very program he grew up in and experienced as an Army kid.

The phase God wants us to attain is a phase called "sold out." "*So likewise, whoever of you does not forsake all that he has cannot be My disciple.*" (Luke 14:33 NKJV) Putting God above everything else in our life is the process of sanctification.

Being sold out means that we do not love our life to the death, "*And they overcame him by the blood of the Lamb and by the word of their testimony, and they did not love their lives to the death.*" (Revelation 12:11 NKJV) It means that we would rather die than deny Jesus. We are completely sold on the fact that God will take care of us no matter the circumstances. The level of commitment is displayed in the believer's actions. Our faith and love for Jesus results in an overwhelming desire to serve the Lord and His people through obedience. Other things don't matter. As Paul states, "*Yet indeed I also count all things loss for the excellence of the knowledge of Christ Jesus my Lord, for whom I have suffered the loss of all things, and count them as rubbish, that I may gain Christ.*" (Philippians 3:8 NKJV)

If we properly think through the logic on being sold out, then it makes sense. To be absent in the body is to be present with Christ. So, losing our earthly life means that we will be with Christ. Why should we fear death? It only means that we will be with Christ and the joy associated with it.

Christianity is hard because people only make it to the stage that their faith will take them. It is like the Peter Principle in leadership which says, "People rise to a level that matches their competency." It is similar in faith. A person's relationship with the Savior will go as far as their faith will take them. People make it to a certain stage and are content or don't realize that Jesus wants to take them further. The Bible talks to this subject. Here Paul is writing about continuing to improve through Christ for what lays ahead in this journey of faith, *"Not that I have already attained, or am already perfected; but I press on, that I may lay hold of that for which Christ Jesus has also laid hold of me."* (Philippians 3:12 NKJV) And Paul points out that God will reveal the upward call of God in Christ Jesus, *"I press toward the goal for the prize of the upward call of God in Christ Jesus. Therefore, let us, as many as are mature, have this mind; and if in anything you think otherwise, God will reveal even this to you."* (Philippians 3:14–15 NKJV)

As we make this journey, we will do well to help others, *"Beloved, you do faithfully whatever you do for the brethren and for strangers, who have borne witness of your love before the church. If you send them forward on their journey in a manner worthy of God, you will do well."* (3 John 1:5–6 NKJV)

Even with all these phases, disciples can only make it so far. Until we reach Heaven, we will still struggle with the flesh and fall short of the sinless perfection that can only come through resurrection. And just like the heroes of faith, we will need to play it straight up until we are made perfect, *"And all these, having obtained a good testimony through faith, did not receive the promise, God having provided something better for us, that they should not be made perfect apart from us."* (Hebrews 11:39–40 NKJV)

It takes faith to believe in the mysteries of God. One of the mysteries is our salvation from our sins. *"God's desire for our life is to accept Him and come to the saving knowledge of His Son"*. (2 Tim 2:4 NKJV) Believing (making the choice) gives God the victory because we have chosen to believe and love Him over Satan and the ways of this world. Our faith enables God to work in our lives. Our faith is the victory, *"For whatever is born of God overcomes the world. And this is the victory that has overcome the world—our faith."* (1 John 5:4 NKJV)

Here is another standard of our faith journey. This is a journey to become Christlike, *"till we all come to the unity of the faith and of the knowledge of the Son of God, to a perfect man, to the measure of the stature of the fullness of Christ."* (Ephesians 4:13 NKJV)

Christianity is hard because the further we go along our faith journey, the further it appears that we must go. We fall miserably short of the Glory of God. We ought to thank our Lord and Savior that He continues to bear with us. Pray for the strength and courage to continue seeking God first.

Devotional – Playing It Straight Up

One of the phrases I use from time to time is "Play it straight up." This means to stay true regardless of the outcome. To give control to God. And stay faithful to Him and His ways. Loving God and others regardless of the circumstances.

To be honest, I am not very good at playing it straight up. I am always planning and looking for a better way. It is in my nature. The sinful nature I was born with. So, to play it straight and give up control takes a lot of faith for me. It takes real trust to let go and have God provide. While I want to believe, my mind rages with all the possibilities that I can use to control the outcome. As I have grown and matured (read: became older), I have learned that the best path is to trust God. *"Therefore, let us, as many as are mature, have this mind; and if in anything you think otherwise, God will reveal even this to you."* (Philippians 3:15 NKJV)

Solomon understood what it meant to play it straight up. After trying "everything under the sun," Solomon sums up all his efforts in Ecclesiastes, *"Let us hear the conclusion of the whole matter: Fear God and keep His commandments, For this is man's all. For God will bring every work into judgment, Including every secret thing, Whether good or evil."* (Ecclesiastes 12:13–14 NKJV)

One cannot determine or know the ways of God. Therefore, we cannot be sure of the outcome. Isaiah quotes the Lord, *"For as the heavens are higher than the earth, so are My ways higher than your ways, And My thoughts than your thoughts."* (Isaiah 55:9 NKJV) We should believe that God is able to exceed our expectation, *"Now to Him who is able to do exceedingly abundantly above all that we ask or think, according to the power that works in us."* (Ephesians 3:20 NKJV) Do we believe it?

"As you do not know what is the way of the wind, Or how the bones grow in the womb of her who is with child, So you do not know the works of God who makes everything." (Ecclesiastes 11:5 NKJV)

Sometimes people want to quit because they think they are going to lose. Or they think that the outcome isn't going to be favorable. The heroes of faith in Hebrews chapter eleven played it straight up. They stayed true to God regardless of the circumstances. *"And all these, having obtained a good testimony through faith, did not receive the promise."* (Heb 11:39 NKJV) They didn't quit even though they didn't receive what they were expecting. They will yet receive it.

In the book of Luke, Jesus is describing the end times. He is describing all these horrible things that humans will experience. And then He states that it will be an opportunity to glorify God, *"But it will turn out for you as an occasion for testimony."* (Luke 21:13 NKJV) This is an example of playing it straight up. Regardless of the circumstances, we will be given an opportunity to glorify Jesus Christ and our Father in heaven, God. The next verse is a key to being able to maintain our head in times of distress. *"Therefore, settle it in your hearts not to meditate beforehand on what you will answer."* (Luke 21:14 NKJV)

I had something settled in my heart prior to going to Afghanistan. There were news reports about beheadings and live burnings on TV. It is a means of intimidation. I had determined beforehand that they would have to cut off my head while I was praising my Lord and Savior Jesus Christ. I wasn't going to struggle to hang onto this life when I know what awaits me in heaven. I was going to use it as an opportunity for testimony. I wanted to play it straight up. God spared me from this ending, and I praise Him for it.

Jesus ends this section in Luke by saying, *"By your patience possess your souls."* (Luke 21:19 NKJV) Possess your soul. This is another way to say play it straight up.

CHAPTER 15

GOD'S WILL

"For this is the will of God, your sanctification."

1 THESSALONIANS 4:3A (NKJV)

Christianity is hard because knowing God's specific will for our life is difficult at best. God's general will for our lives is easier to understand.

God's will for our life is to be in a relationship with Him, *"Behold, the tabernacle of God is with men, and He will dwell with them, and they shall be His people. God Himself will be with them and be their God."* (Revelation 21:3 NKJV) The Bible repeatedly states that God wants to be our God. Here are just a few of them:

"And I will establish My covenant between Me and you and your descendants after you in their generations, for an everlasting covenant, to be God to you and your descendants after you."

(GENESIS 17:7 NKJV)

"I will take you as My people, and I will be your God. Then you shall know that I am the LORD your God."

(EXODUS 6:7A NKJV)

"I will walk among you and be your God, and you shall be My people."

(LEVITICUS 26:12 NKJV)

"He who overcomes shall inherit all things, and I will be his God and he shall be My son."

(REVELATION 21:7 NKJV)

God's will for our life is for God to be first in everything, *"But seek first the kingdom of God and His righteousness, and all these things shall be added to you."*

(MATTHEW 6:33 NKJV)

God's will for our life is to know Him. God's Word is very clear about knowing Him. Jesus prays that knowing God is eternal life, *"And this is eternal life, that they may know You, the only true God, and Jesus Christ whom You have sent."* (John 17:3 NKJV) And Paul states the importance of knowing Jesus, *"For I determined not to know anything among you except Jesus Christ and Him crucified."* (1 Corinthians 2:2 NKJV)

When we know God and the love of His Son, it surpasses knowledge, *"to know the love of Christ which passes knowledge; that you may be filled with all the fullness of God."* (Ephesians 3:19 NKJV) The reason it surpasses knowledge is because it takes faith. Faith surpasses knowledge.

One of the best ways to know God is to read the Bible. God's word is provided to us to equip us for every good work, *"All Scripture is given by inspiration of God, and is profitable for doctrine, for reproof, for correction, for instruction in righteousness that the man of God may be complete, thoroughly equipped for every good work."* (2 Timothy 3:16–17 NKJV) It is also best to read the Bible every day.

Otherwise we become spiritually unfit. This is just like being physically fit. If we don't work out, we will become flabby and out of shape. This applies to our spiritual wellbeing also, *"For bodily exercise profits a little, but godliness is profitable for all things, having promise of the life that now is and of that which is to come."* (1 Timothy 4:8 NKJV)

God's will for our life is to love Him, "*You shall love the LORD your God with all your heart, with all your soul, and with all your strength.*" (Deuteronomy 6:5 NKJV) To know God is to love God. God wants us to love Him with everything He has given us. He has given us our heart, our soul, and our strength. We are only really giving back to Him what he has already given to us. And He tells us how to love "*and walk in love, as Christ also has loved us and given Himself for us.*" (Ephesians 5:2a NKJV)

Loving God comes with a promise that all things will work for good, "*And we know that all things work together for good to those who love God, to those who are the called according to His purpose.*" (Romans 8:28 NKJV)

God's will for our life is to fear Him. There are many places in the Bible where we receive instructions and commands to fear God, "*You shall fear the LORD your God and serve Him.*" (Deuteronomy 6:13 NKJV) The wisest man in the Bible concludes after trying everything in the world, "*Let us hear the conclusion of the whole matter: Fear God and keep His commandments, For this is man's all.*" (Ecclesiastes 12:13 NKJV) The Bible also has many places where it tells us to not fear, "*You must not fear them, for the LORD your God Himself fights for you.*" (Deuteronomy 3:22 NKJV) When we are told to not fear God, it is because He is with us and will fight for us.

God's will for our life is to live for Him. With every decision, there is a choice between God and Satan. We have limited strength to conquer sin or Satan. Satan will have his way with us if we try on our own. If we live in Christ and He is us, then all things are possible. Christ's strength carries the day, not ours, "*I can do all things through Christ who strengthens me.*" (Philippians 4:13 NKJV) Then we are able to live for Him, "*yet for us there is one God, the Father, of whom are all things, and we for Him; and one Lord Jesus Christ, through whom are all things, and through whom we live.*" (1 Corinthians 8:6 NKJV) So, when we accept God's will that we live for Him, then we will do everything to His glory, "*Therefore, whether you eat or drink, or whatever you do, do all to the glory of God.*" (1 Corinthians 10:31 NKJV)

God wants to live in us and through us, "*I have been crucified with*

Christ; it is no longer I who live, but Christ lives in me; and the life which I now live in the flesh I live by faith in the Son of God, who loved me and gave Himself for me." (Galatians 2:20 NKJV) And by living in us and through us, we will live for Him. When Christ is living in us, then we can say, "*I delight to do Your will, O my God, And Your law is within my heart.*" (Psalm 40:8 NKJV) Pray that we all choose to live for God today and every day.

God's will for our life is to be like Him. Even from the beginning we are to represent the image of God, "*So God created man in His own image; in the image of God He created him; male and female He created them.*" (Genesis 1:27 NKJV) Since the fall of man, God has been or is in the process of restoring us to His holiness. This process is called sanctification, "*For this is the will of God, your sanctification: that you should abstain from sexual immorality; that each of you should know how to possess his own vessel in sanctification and honor.*" (1 Thessalonians 4:3–4 NKJV)

There are different levels of sanctification. First, we have been sanctified by the work of Jesus, "*By that will we have been sanctified through the offering of the body of Jesus Christ once for all.*" (Hebrews 10:10 NKJV) Through Christ we are sanctified. Second, we are in the process of being sanctified as Jesus prays to the Father, "*Sanctify them by Your truth. Your word is truth.*" (John 17:17 NKJV) As a believer living in this world, we know we haven't achieved holiness. Therefore, we are in the sanctification process during this life on earth, "*Now may the God of peace Himself sanctify you completely; and may your whole spirit, soul, and body be preserved blameless at the coming of our Lord Jesus Christ.*" (1 Thessalonians 5:23 NKJV) Third, at the appearing of the Lord, we will again be like Him (sanctified and holy), "*Beloved, now we are children of God; and it has not yet been revealed what we shall be, but we know that when He is revealed, we shall be like Him, for we shall see Him as He is.*" (1 John 3:2 NKJV) This was all to say God's will for our life is to be like Him.

God's will for our life is to serve Him. This verse shows many of the ways God wants us to honor Him, "*What does the LORD your God require of you, but to fear the LORD your God, to walk in all His ways and to love*

Him, to serve the LORD your God with all your heart and with all your soul." (Deuteronomy 10:12 NKJV) Faith, fear, obedience, love, and serving are all God's will for our life.

Jesus tells a parable about talents. God has given us talents and we are to use them serving Him. To the servant who produced fruits from his talents, *"his lord said to him, 'Well done, good and faithful servant; you were faithful over a few things, I will make you ruler over many things. Enter into the joy of your lord.'"* (Matthew 25:21 NKJV) To the unprofitable servant and his end, *"cast the unprofitable servant into the outer darkness. There will be weeping and gnashing of teeth."* (Matthew 25:30 NKJV) So, there is a choice to be made with our talents that God has given us. The result of that choice is that we will either be in the joy of the Lord or cast into the outer darkness. God wants us to serve Him with the talents He has given to us.

God wants us to obey and follow Him. Obedience to many means that we needed to follow a whole bunch of rules. This means that the Christian life would be dismal and no fun. Always checking to see if we are obeying the letter of the law. We have been freed from the law, *"For the law of the Spirit of life in Christ Jesus has made me free from the law of sin and death."* (Romans 8:2 NKJV)

We can be a follower of Christ and have fun. This was revolutionary and very freeing. We like to have fun. If we are not having fun, then we are going to find something else to do. Jesus has freed us from the bondage of sin. Jesus freed us so that we can live for Him and serve Him.

Obedience now means that we follow Christ. We do what he tells us to do. The Spirit of God will prompt us to do things. Some of the actions are little, like go talk to a person. Others are big and longer-term actions like serve at a church or go to the mission field. By following and loving Jesus, His commands are now not burdensome, *"For this is the love of God, that we keep His commandments. And His commandments are not burdensome."* (1 John 5:3 NKJV)

Christianity is hard because God's plan for our life may not be what we think it should be. We must align our thinking and submit to His will.

Personal application – God has a plan for my life. I do believe this is the case. But what does that mean? What does that life look like? How will I know it? And the big question, what if I don't like it when I am living that new life? Is that my flesh speaking? Can God take care of my smallest need in ways that I can't envision? My mind reels with these questions. In different phases of my journey, I believed I knew what God wanted me to do in that phase. God's plan for my life at that moment or for that period of time was clear. So, as I journeyed through life, God revealed to me what the next steps were at the time He wanted me to act. I have never received a plan for my "life," only the next step. Maybe that is the way it works, at least for me. This phase has me writing a book. I am being obedient and writing even though I don't think I am worthy or what I am writing will matter.

Here is an example of my questioning God's will for my life. I came up with a plan to retire. I created spreadsheets. Tracked dates and funding. Built a budget. I calculated every possible angle. I have the budget planned out until my late eighties. I built scenarios of if I die early, will my wife be taken care of and whether to take social security early or not. We were well into executing the plan. I was going to take all unknowns out of the plan before retiring. We bought the new house which we call the cabin. The plan was moving along to my pace and schedule. But I believe God has other plans for me and my wife. And He started to intervene.

During my Bible readings, the Spirit would bring passages to my mind for me to ponder. Like the passage about the guy who stored up all his food and said to himself, *I will take some time off*. God calls him a fool and takes his life the next day. (Luke 12:16–21 NKJV) I clearly don't want to be that guy.

Then there is the rich man who is told to go sell everything and follow Jesus. The rich man goes away sad because he keeps all of his stuff. (Matt 10:17–25 NKJV) I don't want to be this guy either. Of course, there is the passage in Acts 5 about my name-sake, Ananias (my grandparents migrated to the US with the name Anania, and just like any family I prefer to think I came from the Ananias in ACTS chapter 9). So, I have always felt a close connection to these specific Bible passages. And again, Ananias and his wife both die immediately for withholding back part of the proceeds selling their house and lying about it.

So, is that the plan for my life? Should I sell everything and work the rest of my life? Then there is this proverb, "*Do not overwork to be rich; Because of your own understanding, cease!*" (Proverbs 23:4 NKJV) Hmmm. Makes me wonder.

I am submitting to the will of God understanding that He can take it all away. I am okay with it because He will take care of me regardless. Everything I have is His. I willfully submit my life to Christ. I am going to follow the next step not knowing where it will lead. I will live in anticipation of how Christ will bless me.

Christianity is hard because the specific will for my life is revealed to me one step at a time. I don't know God's specific plan for my life in its entirety. He hasn't shared it with me, or at least that I am aware of. I only know the next step. He wants me to trust Him with the rest.

There are passages that say it is well for a man to enjoy the fruits of his work. Ecclesiastes calls it a gift of God, "*As for every man to whom God has given riches and wealth, and given him power to eat of it, to receive his heritage and rejoice in his labor—this is the gift of God.*" (Ecclesiastes 5:19 NKJV) The next verse provides some insight into this perplexing situation, "*For he will not dwell unduly on the days of his life, because God keeps him busy with the joy of his heart.*" (Ecclesiastes 5:20 NKJV) First, a key here is that God is involved. Second, it is the joy of the rich man's heart. The joy of his heart is to follow Christ and live for Him. Pray that God will give us that joy today and every day.

Looking further into the joy of the heart lands us in Deuteronomy,

"*Because you did not serve the LORD your God with joy and gladness of heart, for the abundance of everything.*" (Deuteronomy 28:47 NKJV) This section of the Bible is talking about blessings and curses. Obviously, this statement is related to curses. And relates to the rich man question. And just like all things related to faith, it is a matter of the heart. Are we placing God first in our life? The money doesn't mean anything because we don't trust the money—we trust God. God can provide and God can take away. We are only kidding ourselves that we can hold onto anything apart from God.

There is another aspect of this question. Where are we placing our trust? All of society, and what we were taught by the world, says take care of ourselves. But where are we placing our trust—in the money and things or God? One thing the Bible and life teaches us is that God controls everything. So, He can just take it at any given point in time. Or He can also supply it as well.

We should continually seek God's guidance on the matter, "*Come now, you who say, 'Today or tomorrow we will go to such and such a city, spend a year there, buy and sell, and make a profit'; whereas you do not know what will happen tomorrow. For what is your life? It is even a vapor that appears for a little time and then vanishes away. Instead you ought to say, 'If the Lord wills, we shall live and do this or that.' But now you boast in your arrogance. All such boasting is evil.*" (James 4:13–16 NKJV)

And then it says, "*Therefore, to him who knows to do good and does not do it, to him it is sin.*" (James 4:17 NKJV) God looks at the heart and we must stay focused on Him.

God's will for our life is to glorify Him. Jesus paid the price, so we ought to glorify the Father, "*For you were bought at a price; therefore glorify God in your body and in your spirit, which are God's.*" (1 Corinthians 6:20 NKJV) In respect of all that God has and will do for us, we should represent God to other folks, "*Let your light so shine before men, that they may see your good works and glorify your Father in heaven.*" (Matthew 5:16 NKJV) And in the end, we will glorify God. An angel will be preaching the gospel, "*saying with a loud voice 'Fear God and give glory to Him, for the hour of His judgment has come; and worship Him who made heaven and earth, the sea and springs of water.'"* (Revelation 14:7 NKJV)

God's general will for everyone's life is clear: He is our God and we are His people. We are to know, love and fear Him, and eventually be like Him through sanctification. God's plan for our life is to follow Him in obedience, glorify His name, and rest in His goodness and grace, *"and the peace of God, which surpasses all understanding, will guard your hearts and minds through Christ Jesus."* (Philippians 4:7 NKJV)

In conclusion, Christianity is simple if we will only follow the Lord, *"Trust in the LORD with all your heart, and lean not on your own understanding; in all your ways acknowledge Him, and He shall direct your paths. Do not be wise in your own eyes; Fear the LORD and depart from evil."* (Proverbs 3:5–7 NKJV)

Solomon provides the same conclusion, *"Let us hear the conclusion of the whole matter: Fear God and keep His commandments, for this is man's all. For God will bring every work into judgment, including every secret thing, whether good or evil."* (Ecclesiastes12:13–14 NKJV)

A hard part of Christianity is accepting God's will for our life. To let God have complete control, trusting Him and living for Him with all our heart, mind, and soul. Pray that we have that kind of faith and submit to God and our Lord Jesus Christ. May the grace of our Lord Jesus Christ be with you!

9 781400 330973